GREAT AMERICAN

FOR
JAMES BEARD
AND JULIA CHILD,
WHO LIT THE LAMP
AND SHOWED US
THE WAY

COOKING SCHOOLS

GREAT AMERICAN COOKING SCHOOLS

American Food & California Wine
Bountiful Bread: Basics to Brioches
Christmas Feasts from History
Cooking from a Country Kitchen
Cooking of the South
Dim Sum & Chinese One-Dish Meals
Fair Game: A Hunter's Cookbook
Fine Fresh Food—Fast
Fresh Garden Vegetables
Ice Cream & Ices
Microwave Cooking: Meals in Minutes
Old-Fashioned Desserts
Omelettes & Soufflés
Pasta! Cooking It, Loving It
Quiche & Pâté
Romantic & Classic Cakes
Soups & Salads
Successful Parties: Simple & Elegant

Old-Fashioned Desserts

RICHARD SAX

ILLUSTRATED BY MARC ROSENTHAL

IRENA CHALMERS COOKBOOKS, INC. • NEW YORK

This is for Mick,
who has wonderful taste,
and who eats desserts for breakfast

IRENA CHALMERS COOKBOOKS, INC.

PUBLISHER
Irena Chalmers

Managing Editor
Jean Atcheson

Sales and Marketing Director
Diane J. Robbins

Series Design
Helen Berinsky

Cover Design
Milton Glaser
Karen Skelton, *Associate Director*

Cover Photography
Matthew Klein

Designer for this book
Mary Ann Joulwan

Editor for this book
Jean Atcheson

Typesetting
Acu-Type Services, Clinton, CT

Printing
Lucas Litho., Inc., Baltimore, MD

Editorial Office
23 East 92nd Street
New York, NY 10028
(212) 289-3105

Sales Office
P.O. Box 988
Denton, NC 27239
(800) 334-8128 or
(704) 869-4518 (NC)

ISBN #0-941034-18-6

© 1983 by Richard Sax. All rights reserved.
Printed and published in the United States of America
by Irena Chalmers Cookbooks, Inc.

LIBRARY OF CONGRESS
CATALOG NO.: 83-071446
   Sax, Richard.
      Old-fashioned desserts.
   New York, NY: Chalmers, Irena Cookbooks, Inc.
84 p.
E D C B A   7 6 5 4 3   695/17

The quotation on page 43 is from *Speak to the Earth*
by Rachel Peden, published by Alfred A. Knopf, Inc.
in 1974; reprinted with permission.

Contents

Acknowledgments 8

Introduction 9
A Few Notes on Ingredients 10

Recipes

Fruit Desserts 13
   Baked Stuffed Apples 14
     Raisin-Nut Stuffing 14
   Blueberry Grunt 15
     Dumpling Topping 15
   Blackberry Cobbler 16
     Buttermilk Biscuit Topping 16
   Cranberry-Apple Crumble 18
     Crumble Topping 18
   Pear Pandowdy 19
   Plum Dumplings 20

   Biscuit Dough 20
   Prune Clafoutis 21
   Warm Pear Charlotte 22
   Lime Syllabub 24
   Plum Fool 25
   Johanne's Poached Pears with
     Zinfandel and Mascarpone 26
     Mascarpone Cream 26
   Dried Fruit Compote 27

Puddings 29
   Pound Cake Pudding 30
   Orange Bread Pudding 31
   Cabinet Pudding 32
   Little Tapioca Puddings
     with Caramel 33

Crème Brûlée 34
Creamy Rice Pudding 36
  Vanilla Custard Sauce
  (Crème Anglaise) 36
Cornmeal Pudding with Hard Sauce . . . 37
Noodle Kugel
    (JEWISH NOODLE PUDDING) 37
Steamed Pumpkin Pudding with
  Ginger-Lemon Cream 38
A Note on Chocolate 40
Chocolate Soufflé
  The Quilted Giraffe 40
Brandy Chocolate Sauce 41

Pies & Tarts 43
Two-Layer Lemon Pie 44

Country Peach Pie 45
Double-Berry Lattice Pie 46
The Coach House Pecan Pie 48
  The Coach House Rich Pastry 48
Butterscotch Cream Pie 49
  Graham Cracker Crust 49
Edna Lewis's Raspberry Pie 50
  Edna Lewis's Lard Pastry 51
Italian Rice and Ricotta Pie 52
Pumpkin Soufflé Pie 53
Sweet Potato Pie with
  Almond Crunch Topping 54
  Mrs. Brown's Flake Pie Dough 55
Hungarian Cheese Tart 55
Prune Mirliton with Grand Marnier
  (A NUT CAKE FROM NORMANDY) 56
Ruth's Rustic Autumn Tart 57

Alsatian Apple Tart with
  Macaroon Crunch Topping 58
Galette Bressane (GEORGES BLANC'S
  CRÈME FRAÎCHE TART) 60
Caramel Walnut Tart 61

Cakes & Cookies 63
Peach-Pecan Upside-Down Cake 64
Chocolate Almond Cake 65
Ligita's Latvian Apple Cake 66
Ginger Cake 67
Rich Gingerbread 68
  Chunky Applesauce 69
Rich Soft Spice Cake 69
Sour Cream Kuchen with
  Two Toppings 70
  Kuchen Dough 70

Plum-Streusel Topping 71
  Bienenstich (Bee-Sting) Glaze 71
Buttermilk Shortcake 72
Chocolate-Flecked Angel Food Cake 74
Semolina Cake with Apples 75
Jewish Honey Cake (LEKACH) 76
Périgord Pumpkin-Rice Cake 76
Crisp Macadamia Wafers 78
Rich Macaroon Squares 79
Hermits 80
Quaresemali Biscuits 81

Basic Preparations 82
Basic Pie Pastry 82
Sweet Tart Pastry 83
Cookie Crust 83
Crème Fraîche 84

Acknowledgments

I want to thank a few of the people who helped make this book such a joy to work on. First, Irena Chalmers, who suggested the topic, and her staff, who brought the book into being. Lorna Sass was more than generous with her library and her knowledge, and often welcomed me to her home with hot soup, fresh dates, and other treats. Elizabeth Schneider Colchie went out of her way to offer useful advice and information. Chris Styler and Helen Witty both offered helpful information when I approached them with questions.

Many home cooks inspired me with their dedication to quality in the kitchen, and they are referred to below. I thank them all.

For diligent help with the manuscript, I thank Diane Hodges and Nina Fairbanks.

A special word for Ruth Cousineau, a terrific cook and friend. Ruth helped test all the recipes, and for all the times she brought some special bit of expertise to her work, or chided me with "Are you *sure* this is good enough to be included in the book?" I give her thanks and a big hug. The fact that I'm as pleased as I am with this material is due largely to Ruth.

Introduction

If you are looking for elegant desserts and *pâtisserie*, you have opened the wrong book. Lots of us are rediscovering the joys of cooking the way our grandmothers did, and with good reason.

Desserts aren't exactly enjoying an honored reputation these days. According to the French critics Gault and Millau, we Americans have "a nearly childish weakness for sweets in general." One of my wisest teachers, a baker named Carlo Bussetti, often bemoans today's sad state of American commercial baking. "They use lousy ingredients," he says, shaking his head sadly, "then put plenty of sugar in it, and people think it's good. But where can you get a good piece of Danish?"

At *home*, that's where. Even for the diet-conscious, there's nothing wrong with enjoying a freshly made pie, cobbler or pudding—if it's a good one.

This book is by no means an exhaustive compendium of the world's old-fashioned desserts. Rather, it's a collection of recipes which I like, and which represent a certain type of fine home cooking, both in America and elsewhere. Many of them are updated versions of dessert recipes from classic cookbooks. Others have been given to me by superb home cooks from all over the United States, and other recipes were developed especially for this collection. All have been streamlined and updated, without losing that elusive old-fashioned flavor.

In my cooking classes, I often demonstrate techniques, and then offer the students a table full of fresh ingredients, so they can create their own dishes using the techniques they have learned. I usually suggest alternatives and variations to a recipe, so that students (and readers) can bring their own tastes to their cooking. While dessert recipes do require a bit more precision than most, I believe that your cooking can really become a gift from your heart when it truly reflects *you*. This book has been a pleasure to work on, and it would make me very happy indeed to learn that you had transformed a recipe into something of your own.

A FEW NOTES ON INGREDIENTS

I'm not a believer in exotica, though you should always seek out the best ingredients you can find. This is especially true of the recipes which call for fresh fruits. Here are a few notes on ingredients called for in the recipes:

BUTTER—I always use top-quality unsalted butter.

EGGS—All recipes have been tested for Large eggs.

FLOUR—Whenever flour is called for, it means all-purpose flour, preferably unbleached.

NUTS—Try to find a reliable source for impeccably fresh nuts. Nuts keep best in tightly sealed containers in the freezer or refrigerator.

SPICES—Throw away any spices you have had for a year or longer, and buy small quantities, so you will always have the flavors of fresh spices in your cooking. An electric coffee grinder or mortar and pestle will do a good job of grinding whole spices.

BROWN SUGAR—I prefer dark brown sugar, for its deep flavor. Granulated brown sugar can be substituted.

MOLASSES—You can measure molasses (or honey) easily by first coating the measuring cup lightly with vegetable oil.

BUTTERMILK—You will note that I have used buttermilk a lot, especially in biscuit doughs (for cobblers, and so on). It gives a light texture and excellent flavor. If it's more convenient, you can substitute yogurt, thinned with milk.

CRÈME FRAÎCHE—In a few recipes, I have called for this luxuriously thick, slightly sour French cream. You can ferment an approximation of this at home (see page 84); or you can always substitute heavy cream, to which you have added a spoonful of sour cream, for flavor.

GRATED CITRUS ZEST—I find it easiest to use the small handled tool called a zester for this. As the zester is drawn across the citrus skin, it removes the zest in long strands, which can then be chopped quickly with a knife.

[Fruit desserts such as deep-dish pies, cobblers, grunts, and pandowdies are] the serve-in-bowl desserts practical for every day, long on fruit and short on pastry. They've always been the farm woman's favorite way to salvage fruit that might otherwise be wasted when the orchard yields a bumper crop.

—*from* Farm Journal's
Complete Pie Cookbook

---

*I*t is ironic that, while simple desserts made with fresh fruits typify good American home cooking, there are few recipes for them in old American cookbooks. Perhaps, as James Beard surmises in *American Cookery*, it was assumed that homemakers would know how to prepare them. In an article in *Gourmet* magazine called "Grunts, Slumps, Cobblers, and Pandowdies," Elizabeth Schneider Colchie notes that "early New Englanders were, in fact, so fond of these juicy dishes that they often served them . . . for breakfast, . . . and it was not until the late 19th century that they became primarily desserts."

This brief collection includes many old-time favorites, and there's no reason why we can't enjoy them for breakfast, too.

Fruit
Desserts

Baked Stuffed Apples

There is probably no dessert more "down home" than a baked apple warm from the oven, served with thick fresh cream. But baked apples can take many guises, some quite elaborate: At Le Pavillon, in New York, apple halves were poached in a honey syrup, stuffed with fruits, and baked with a rum-spiked pastry cream and cake crumbs. Scandinavian recipes find the apples filled with rich almond paste and served with custard, while in Italy, whole pears are baked with syrup until their glazed skins are crinkled and golden. In this raisin-and-nut-filled version, flavorful whole-wheat bread-crumbs coat each neat apple "package."

**4 large apples, e.g.,
    Granny Smiths
Fresh lemon juice, as needed**

STUFFING:
**⅓ cup walnuts or almonds,
    coarsely chopped
¼ cup raisins or currants
¼ cup honey, or as needed
4 tablespoons unsalted butter,
    melted
⅓ cup breadcrumbs, whole wheat
    if available
2 tablespoons sugar
Water, as needed**

Preheat the oven to 375 degrees.

Core the apples, cutting a cavity about 1 inch wide but leaving the bottoms intact. Peel the skin around the stem end to expose a ring of flesh about 2½ inches wide. Rub the cut surfaces of the apples with lemon juice to prevent discoloration.

To make the stuffing, combine the nuts, raisins, 2 tablespoons of the honey, a little melted butter and a few drops of lemon juice in a small bowl. Stir to blend, adding a bit more honey if needed to bind the mixture. Gently pack the stuffing into the cavities in the apples, mounding it slightly.

Brush the exposed flesh of the apples with melted butter. Holding each apple over a bowl, press a layer of breadcrumbs onto the buttered flesh, shaking off the excess. Arrange the apples in a shallow baking dish. Place a small cap of foil over the stuffing (this prevents the raisins from burning) and prick the skin of each apple in 2 or 3 places. Drizzle the breadcrumbs with the remaining honey and melted butter. Pour about ¼ inch of hot water into the baking dish.

Bake the apples, basting them once or twice with the juices in the dish for the first 10 minutes. Continue to bake until the apples are just tender and the crumbs are lightly toasted, about 25 to 30 minutes in all. Do not overbake; the centers of the apples should offer some resistance when a small knife is inserted.

Serve warm or cold, with the syrup in the dish, and heavy cream, if you like.

Blueberry Grunt

Makes 6 servings

A grunt (whose name, writes Elizabeth Schneider Colchie, is thought by some New Englanders to be approximately the sound the berries make as they stew) is similar to a cobbler, except that it is simmered, rather than baked. As it cooks, usually in a cast-iron skillet, the biscuit dough sets to form soft dumplings.

Sometimes, a grunt is called a slump (of which Louisa May Alcott was so fond that she named her house in Concord, Massachusetts, "Apple Slump"); Southern cooks prepare a similar recipe called "blackberry dumplins."

Helen Witty, a food writer wise in the ways of traditional home desserts, recently compared the grunt's tender topping to a "quilt," a comparison I find most inviting.

About 5 cups (2 boxes)
  blueberries, picked over
1 tablespoon lemon juice
¾ cup sugar
1 tablespoon cornstarch
Pinch cinnamon

DUMPLING TOPPING:
1 cup flour
2 tablespoons sugar
1 teaspoon baking powder
½ teaspoon baking soda
Pinch salt
2 tablespoons melted butter
½ cup buttermilk, or as needed

Whipped cream, heavy cream or
  ice cream

Toss the berries with the lemon juice in a wide, non-corrosive skillet or flameproof shallow baking dish. Stir together the cornstarch, sugar and cinnamon in a small bowl, and stir this mixture gently into the berries until combined. Cover the pan and bring to a boil.

To make the dumpling topping, sift the flour, sugar, baking powder, baking soda and salt into a mixing bowl. Gently stir in the melted butter, and then enough of the buttermilk to make a very soft dough. Stir just to combine; do not overmix.

As soon as the berries begin to boil, uncover the pan, lower the heat, and drop rounded tablespoonfuls of the topping onto the berries, spacing them evenly. Cover the pan tightly and simmer for 15 minutes without lifting the lid. Check to see that the dumplings have set; cool slightly.

Serve warm in bowls, with whipped cream, heavy cream or ice cream.

Blackberry Cobbler

Basically, a cobbler consists of a layer of fruit baked with a crust, though there is little agreement. The crust may be pastry, biscuit or bread dough.

Here is a simple and delectable version, made with a light buttermilk biscuit dough, which I think typifies the genre nicely. One of my most lasting memories in testing these recipes is of a berry cobbler enjoyed on a hot summer night with friends in Rhode Island. The thin fruit juices mingled with lightly whipped cream, and we lapped up every last drop.

Some cooking tips: Bringing the fruit mixture to a boil first will help the cornstarch to cook thoroughly, avoiding a starchy taste. For tender results, don't overhandle the biscuit dough. You might like to try this recipe with other berries or fruits, or a combination.

4½-5 cups (2 boxes) blackberries, picked over
1 tablespoon lemon juice
¾ cup sugar, or more if the berries are very tart
1 tablespoon cornstarch
Large pinch cinnamon

BUTTERMILK BISCUIT TOPPING:
1 cup flour
5 tablespoons sugar
1 teaspoon baking powder
½ teaspoon baking soda
½ teaspoon salt
3 tablespoons unsalted butter, chilled
1 egg yolk
⅓ cup buttermilk (approximately)

Whipped cream, heavy cream or ice cream

Preheat the oven to 425 degrees. Butter a shallow baking dish such as a 6-by-10-inch rectangular dish, a 9-inch pie plate, or another dish of similar size.

Place the berries and lemon juice in a saucepan. Stir together the sugar, cornstarch and cinnamon in a small bowl. Gently toss this mixture with the berries until combined.

To make the topping, sift together the flour, 3 tablespoons of the sugar, the baking powder, baking soda and the salt. Cut in the butter until the mixture is coarsely crumbled. Put the egg yolk in a 1-cup measure, and stir in enough buttermilk to measure a generous ⅓ cup. Use a fork to stir the liquid into the dry ingredients gently, just until combined to form a very soft dough.

Scrape the dough onto a lightly floured board. With floured fingertips, pat the dough out gently until it is ½ inch thick. Use a round cutter or a knife to cut the dough into round or diamond shapes.

Bring the berry mixture to a boil, stirring gently; transfer to the prepared baking dish. Gently lay the dough shapes onto the berries, spacing them evenly. Sprinkle the remaining 2 tablespoons of sugar over the top and bake in the preheated oven until the biscuits are lightly golden, about 25 minutes. Cool slightly.

Serve warm in bowls, with whipped cream, heavy cream or ice cream.

Cranberry-Apple Crumble

Makes 8 servings

The crumble, homey British cousin to our crisp and Brown Betty, is named for its rich, shortbread-like oat topping. I have developed this recipe with cranberries, which we use in desserts all too seldom. I once worked with a Parisian pâtissier who made beautiful cranberry tarts (with imported American cranberries); he was shocked when I told him that we usually eat the berries with turkey.

Charles Dickens, visiting Boston in 1842, commented, "In our private room the cloth could not, for any earthly consideration, have been laid for dinner without a huge glass dish of cranberries in the middle of the table . . . ."

Try this crumble with vanilla ice cream.

1 pound cranberries, picked over and rinsed (about 1 quart)
1½ cups sugar
3 tablespoons cornstarch
3 sweet apples (e.g., Golden Delicious) peeled, cored and sliced
Juice and grated zest of 1 orange

TOPPING:
8 tablespoons (4 ounces) cold unsalted butter, cut up
¾ cup brown sugar
¾ cup oatmeal
¾ cup flour
Vanilla ice cream

Preheat the oven to 375 degrees. Butter a 9½- or 10-inch pie dish.

Stir together half of the cranberries, the sugar and the cornstarch in a saucepan. Bring the mixture to a boil and remove from the heat.

Add the remaining cranberries, apples, orange juice and zest to the saucepan, stirring. Pour the mixture into the prepared pie dish.

To make the topping, cut together the butter, brown sugar, oatmeal and flour in a mixing bowl or food processor until crumbly. Spread this mixture over the fruit. Place the baking dish in the oven on a sheet of aluminum foil to catch any drips. Bake until brown, about 35 minutes.

Serve warm or at room temperature, with vanilla ice cream, if you like.

Pear Pandowdy

A pandowdy finds sliced fruit, usually apples, baked with a pastry crust, which is cut up and pressed into the fruit for the last few minutes' baking time. Some versions place the fruit on top of a layer of bread dough, and some invert the dessert before serving. When topped with breadcrumbs, the pandowdy becomes a Brown Betty.

The word pandowdy is of hazy origin; one New England cookbook calls the process of cutting up the dough "dowdying." And according to Ms. Colchie, a pandowdy was often baked all night in an extinguished oven, to be served warm for breakfast.

This simple pear version is sweetened with maple syrup, a characteristic New England flavoring.

7 firm-ripe pears, peeled,
   cored and sliced ½ inch thick
   (about 6-7 cups)
2 tablespoons fresh lemon juice
½ cup pure maple syrup
Large pinch ground cloves
A few gratings of fresh
   nutmeg (or ¼ teaspoon ground)
1 tablespoon unsalted butter
½ recipe Basic Pie Pastry
   (see page 82)
1 tablespoon cream or milk
1-2 tablespoons sugar
Ice cream, heavy cream or
   whipped cream

Preheat the oven to 400 degrees. Butter a 9- or 9½-inch pie plate, or other shallow baking dish.

Toss the sliced pears with the lemon juice in a mixing bowl, to prevent discoloration. Add the maple syrup, cloves and nutmeg, and toss to combine. Place the pears in the buttered dish, smooth over gently and dot with butter.

Roll the pastry on a lightly floured surface until it is ⅛ inch thick, and lay it gently over the pears. Trim flush with the edges of the dish. Brush the pastry with cream or milk, then sprinkle with sugar. Cut several steam vents in the pastry.

Bake until the pastry is lightly golden, about 40 minutes. Remove the pandowdy from the oven and cut the pastry into 1-inch squares. Use a spatula to press the squares into the pear filling (this is called "dowdying").

Return to the oven and bake again until golden brown, about 10 to 15 minutes longer. Serve warm in bowls with ice cream, heavy cream or whipped cream.

Plum Dumplings

Fruit dumplings are a widespread tradition that has nearly disappeared. Hungarians boil plums wrapped in a potato dough, then serve them with plenty of buttery breadcrumbs. This simple dumpling, baked in biscuit dough, can also be prepared with ripe apples, nectarines or peaches.

4 ripe plums, stems removed, halved neatly, and pitted

½ cup brown sugar, or more (depending on the plums' sweetness)

4 tablespoons cold butter, cut into bits

Pinch cinnamon or allspice

BISCUIT DOUGH:

2 cups flour

¼ cup sugar, plus about 2 tablespoons for topping

2 teaspoons baking powder

½ teaspoon salt

6 tablespoons unsalted butter, chilled and cut into bits

⅓ cup milk, plus more as needed

Small amount egg white, beaten 2 or 3 times with a fork

Preheat the oven to 400 degrees.

Set out the plums on a work surface, hollows up. Cut together the brown sugar, butter and cinnamon in a small bowl until crumbly. Tuck this mixture into the hollows of the plums, dividing it evenly among them.

To make the biscuit dough, stir together the flour, sugar, baking powder and salt in a bowl, then cut in the butter until crumbly. Stir in the milk very gently, using a fork, adding just enough for a soft, but not sticky, dough. Gather the dough together and very gently roll or pat it out on a lightly floured surface to make a rectangle a little less than ½ inch thick. Brush the surface very lightly with egg white (this prevents the inside of the dough from becoming soggy), then cut into 8 squares.

Place a plum half, stuffing side up, in the center of each dough square. Gather up the corners of each square and join them at the top center, pinching edges and corners together gently so that the plum is completely covered. (If the dough does not stick together easily, brush the corners with a little cold water.) Place the dumplings on a baking sheet with low sides, brush each lightly with milk, and sprinkle with sugar. Bake in the preheated oven until the dumplings are golden and the plums are tender when poked, about 35 minutes.

Cool the dumplings in their pan on a rack, then serve them warm with heavy cream or vanilla ice cream.

Prune Clafoutis

This rustic fruit-filled pancake is a traditional farmhouse dessert from Limousin, the region in central France which is famed for the oak barrels used to age wine. Clafoutis are most frequently made with ripe cherries, which have a short season; this one, made with Armagnac-steeped prunes, can be prepared all year long. Serve the hearty clafoutis warm, as it will become denser once it cools.

1 cup pitted prunes, quartered,
   soaked in ⅓ cup Armagnac or
   other brandy
¾ cups flour
1 cup confectioners' sugar
Pinch salt
4 eggs, lightly beaten
3 tablespoons plus 1 teaspoon
   unsalted butter, melted and
   cooled slightly
1 cup milk, heated to lukewarm
1½ teaspoons pure vanilla extract
Confectioners' sugar, as needed
Crème fraîche (see page 84)
   or heavy cream

Preheat the oven to 375 degrees. Generously butter a shallow baking dish, such as a 10-inch pie plate.

Soak the prunes in the brandy for at least 1 hour, preferably longer.

Combine the flour, confectioners' sugar and salt in a mixing bowl. Add the eggs, one at a time, mixing gently but thoroughly with a wooden spoon.

Stir in the butter, then the milk. Drain the brandy into the batter and arrange the prune pieces in the baking dish. Pour the batter over the prunes. (The batter can be strained if it is very lumpy, but a few lumps won't hurt.)

Bake in the preheated oven until puffed, golden and set in the center, about 35 minutes. Cool the clafoutis briefly, then sprinkle it with confectioners' sugar and serve warm with crème fraîche or heavy cream.

Warm Pear Charlotte

The term "charlotte" is used for both a warm fruit dessert baked in a bread-lined mold, and for a cold Bavarian cream encircled with ladyfingers. Both are traditional French family desserts, and both are made in the high-sided metal mold called a moule à charlotte.

There is, according to Elizabeth Ayrton in The Cookery of England, *some doubt about the word itself. In 15th-century recipes, "charlet," made with pork or veal, meant* chair laitée, *or meat cooked in milk, often almond milk. Others say that the term was a corruption (perhaps by Carême) of the Hebrew* schalet, *a sweet spiced puree of dried fruit coated with a crisp crust.*

Wherever its name came from, this recipe, based on one from Monique Guillaume, is a nice way to enjoy the intense flavor of ripe pears.

**7 firm-ripe medium-size pears
(about 3 pounds), peeled,
quartered and cored**
Juice of 1 lemon
**12-16 slices whole-wheat or
white bread, crusts removed**
**12 tablespoons (6 ounces)
unsalted butter, melted**
¼ cup sugar
1 teaspoon grated nutmeg
Grated zest of 1 lemon
12-ounce jar apricot preserves
**6 tablespoons brandy or pear
eau-de-vie**
1 cup cream, lightly whipped

Preheat the oven to 400 degrees.

Chop the pears into coarse chunks. Place them in a bowl, toss with lemon juice to prevent discoloration, and set them aside.

Cut 6 slices of the bread in long, thin triangles, and the remaining slices in long, thin rectangular strips. Set the bread pieces aside.

Heat 2 tablespoons of the melted butter in a large skillet. Add the pears (work in batches, if necessary), toss, and steam, covered, until the pears are softened, about 6 minutes. Then uncover the pan, add the sugar, nutmeg and lemon zest and toss everything together over moderate heat. Cook for another 4 minutes or so, uncovered, until the pears are soft and have formed a dry, chunky mixture. Remove the pan from the heat.

While the pears are cooking, prepare the baking dish. Choose a 1½-quart charlotte mold, soufflé dish or other baking dish. Dip half of the bread triangles into the melted butter, and arrange them, points facing the center, in the bottom of the dish. Dip the rectangular strips of bread into the melted butter and arrange the strips around the sides of the mold, overlapping them slightly.

Place half of the pear mixture in the mold, spreading the bread outwards as you do so. Add about a third of the apricot preserves, then sprinkle with a tablespoon or two of the brandy. Add the remaining pears, another third of the preserves, and another tablespoon or so of brandy (reserve the remaining preserves and brandy). Dip

remaining bread triangles into the butter, arrange on top of the mold (points in), and sprinkle the bread with another spoonful of brandy. Put the mold on a baking sheet in the preheated oven, immediately lower the heat to 375 degrees, and bake for 30 minutes. If, before the time is up, the top pieces of bread are getting too brown, cover the mold with foil.

Meanwhile, melt the remaining third of the preserves over low heat, strain, and add the remaining brandy.

When the charlotte is ready, remove it from the oven and place on a cooling rack. Allow to cool for about 5 minutes in the mold, then invert onto a serving platter and let cool for another few minutes. Remove the mold carefully and brush the charlotte with the preserves. Serve warm in wedges, passing whipped cream on the side.

Lime Syllabub

One of the oldest traditional English cream desserts, syllabub makes a light, tart finish to a meal. Elizabeth David calls it a "fragile whip of cream contained in a little glass."

Originally, syllabub was a drink made by placing a deep bowl of wine directly under a cow; the milk would form a fine froth as it was drawn directly into the wine. According to Elizabeth Ayrton, Charles II was so fond of this rich drink that he kept cows in St. James's Park in case he became thirsty during a stroll. The word itself, Dorothy Hartley tells us in her Food in England, *is derived from "Sill," a part of the Champagne country, and "bub," common Elizabethan slang for a bubbling drink, and later, by association, a belly.*

This version is an example of the "everlasting," or firmer syllabub, which is eaten with a spoon, and can be prepared in advance. It is based on Eliza Acton's "Very Superior Whipped Syllabub," from her Modern Cookery, *published in 1878.*

Syllabub was included in the first cookbook published in America, The Compleat Housewife; or accomplish'd gentlewoman's companion, *written by E. [Eliza?] Smith in 1742. Eliza Acton notes that syllabubs are "considered less wholesome without a portion of brandy." You will note that I have duly included it here.*

Cooking tip: *Have patience in beating the wine-cream mixture. Our cream is not as thick as the English double cream, but it will thicken nicely.*

**Grated zest and juice of
    2 limes**
½ cup dry sherry
3 tablespoons brandy
½ cup sugar
1 cup heavy cream, chilled
**Additional lime zest, cut in
    fine julienne strips**

Combine the lime zest and juice with the sherry, 1 tablespoon of the brandy and the sugar in a noncorrosive mixing bowl. Allow to steep at least 1 hour.

Begin to beat the mixture with a whisk or electric mixer. Very gradually add the cream in a thin stream. Continue to beat; after a few minutes the mixture will thicken and then become light and fluffy. When the mixture is very thick and forms soft peaks (but is not completely stiff), beat in the remaining 2 tablespoons of brandy.

Spoon gently into tall glasses and chill. Serve decorated with julienne strips of lime.

Plum Fool

A fool is nothing but a mixture of sweetened cooked fruit and thick cream. It belongs to the family of whimsically named English cream desserts that includes trifles and syllabubs (opposite). The origin of the word fool is a matter of some dispute; it has been maintained that it is derived from the French fouler *(to crush), which might make sense. The* Oxford English Dictionary, *however, refutes this, indicating that the name suggests something silly—a quotation from Florio in 1598 refers to "a kind of clouted cream called a foole or a trifle in English."*

In 1747, Hannah Glasse outlined a recipe for gooseberry fool in her Art of Cookery; *this is still one of the most popular English fools. In some recipes, custard replaces the cream, but cream is best.*

There is a bit less cream in this fool than usual (equal proportions of cream and fruit are traditional), and I have kept it in separate layers, rather than folding everything together. Feel free to adjust this recipe to your own taste, and choose an attractive glass bowl for serving.

2 pounds ripe red plums (9-12), stoned and sliced
½ cup red-currant jelly
⅓-½ cup brown sugar (depending on the plums' sweetness)
3-inch strip of orange peel
1 cinnamon stick
1 cup heavy cream, or 1 cup crème fraîche (see page 84) plus 2 tablespoons milk, chilled
½ teaspoon pure vanilla extract
Toasted almonds, for decoration

Place the plum slices in a heavy saucepan with the currant jelly, brown sugar, orange peel and cinnamon stick. Bring to a boil, stirring occasionally. Boil gently, uncovered, for about 12 to 15 minutes, until the plums are very tender, mashing some of the slices against the side of the pan as they cook. When the plums are tender, remove the pan from the heat, and allow to cool slightly.

Mash some more of the slices; about a quarter of the slices should remain intact. Cool completely, then remove the orange peel and cinnamon stick. (Some people put the fruit through a food mill; I like to leave the skins in.) Chill.

Whip the cream until it mounds gently, and add the vanilla. Layer the plum mixture and cream alternately in a glass serving bowl, beginning with a layer of plums and ending with a layer of cream. Decorate with toasted almonds.

Johanne's Poached Pears with Zinfandel and Mascarpone

Johanne Killeen, an innovative chef and photographer, has shared cooking ideas with me for years. She and her husband, George, served me this beautifully composed fruit dessert at their restaurant in Providence, Rhode Island, and I asked for the recipe on the spot. Try to locate the wickedly smooth mascarpone cheese at an Italian market; cream cheese is a good substitute.

Cooking tip: *Any leftover wine syrup can be reused in fruit salads.*

4 firm-ripe pears
1 bottle Zinfandel wine
¾-1 cup sugar, brown or white
(the amount varies depending
on sweetness of the fruit and
the fruitiness of the wine)

MASCARPONE CREAM:
1 cup mascarpone cheese, or
softened cream cheese
1 cup ricotta cheese
¼ cup sugar
1 to 2 tablespoons Poire William
eau-de-vie (pear brandy) or
other brandy

⅔-1 cup heavy cream, whipped
until nearly stiff and
flavored with a few drops
of vanilla

Peel the pears, leaving the stems on. Slice off just enough from the bottom of each pear so it will stand upright. Arrange the pears in a saucepan in which they fit compactly. Pour the wine over, adding water, if necessary, to cover the fruit. Add the sugar, then cover with a round of parchment or wax paper so the fruit will not discolor. Bring to a boil, then simmer until the pears are just firm-tender. Cool the fruit in the liquid.

Remove the pears with a slotted spoon to a dish, spoon a little of the wine syrup over them and cover to keep moist. Leave at room temperature or chill, as you prefer.

Boil the wine syrup from the pears over medium-high heat until reduced to a syrupy consistency; it will probably need to be reduced to one-third or one-half of its volume. Cool the syrup.

To make the mascarpone cream, blend the mascarpone or cream cheese in a food processor or with a whisk just until smooth. Add the ricotta and blend just until the curds disappear, no longer. Add the sugar and brandy and blend just until incorporated. (Overblending will make the mixture too watery.) Have this mixture at room temperature at serving time.

When you are ready to serve, spread a pool of the cheese mixture on each of 4 plates. Spoon some of the whipped cream into each pool's center. Gently push an upright pear into each "cloud" of whipped cream, and drizzle some of the wine syrup down the sides of each pear.

Dried Fruit Compote

Makes about 6 cups

Although fruit compotes can be found in several cuisines—the 1887 New England Cook Book *includes a compote of gooseberries—they are an almost obligatory conclusion to Jewish holiday meals. "You can use almost anything, as long as you cook it within an inch of its life," says my friend Jonathan the lawyer.*

This colorful compote, with a rich wine syrup, is a pleasant accompaniment to a soft dessert such as a mousse; just be sure not to overcook the fruits.

12-16 black peppercorns
12-16 white peppercorns
12 allspice berries
3-inch strip orange peel
2-to-3-inch strip lemon peel
12 ounces (about 2 cups)
  pitted prunes
8-9 ounces (about 1¾ cups)
  dried apricots
8 ounces (about 1⅓ cups)
  small dried figs
1¼ cups dry Madeira or sherry
½ cup water
¼ cup honey
1 cinnamon stick

Tie the peppercorns, allspice and citrus peels into a small cheesecloth bag. Combine the spices in their bag with all the remaining ingredients in a large saucepan and bring to a boil over moderate heat, stirring occasionally. Reduce the heat, cover and simmer gently until the fruit is nearly tender, about 4 to 5 minutes; do not overcook.

Transfer to serving dish and let cool. Discard the cheesecloth bag. Serve the compote at room temperature.

Blessed be he that invented pudding, for it is a Manna that hits the Palates of all sortes of People.

—M. MISSON, writing in the
early 18th century

---

*J*ust a few of the fanciful names for old-fashioned puddings: Jam roly-poly, half-pay pudding, whim-wham, Monday's pudding, silver-and-gold pudding, flummery, tipsy cake, tipsy parson, hasty pudding, spotted dick, lemon fluff, maids of honour, trifle, tansy pudding, bird's nest pudding, apple porcupine, gold belly pudding, apple-after-the-pig, grateful pudding, general satisfaction pudding, plum duff and kickshaws. (This last was a favorite at 16th- and 17th-century feasts; the name is derived from the French *quelque chose*, meaning "something," and the pudding was, apparently, any mixture of many things together.)

Puddings

Pound Cake Pudding

Makes 10 to 12 servings

This is a wonderfully smooth custard, which I once concocted while home alone, recovering from an illness. For me custards are the ultimate "comfort foods."

5-6 ounces pound cake (slightly stale), preferably homemade
3 cups milk
7 eggs
1 egg yolk
¾ cup sugar
Pinch salt
5 teaspoons pure vanilla extract

Preheat the oven to 350 degrees. Bring a kettle of water to a boil; set it aside, off the heat.

Trim the crusts from the cake, using a serrated knife. Cut the cake into ¼-inch slices. Arrange on the bottom and around sides of a 1-quart baking dish, such as a soufflé dish. Set the baking dish in a roasting pan and set aside.

Scald the milk in a medium-sized saucepan. Meanwhile, combine the eggs, egg yolk, sugar and salt in a large bowl and whisk until smooth. Gradually whisk in the hot milk, then the vanilla. Strain the mixture into the cake-lined baking dish. Let stand at room temperature about 15 minutes.

Place the dish in its pan in the preheated oven and pour enough boiling water into the roasting pan to come halfway up the sides of the pudding in its dish. Bake until the center of the pudding is set and its top is lightly golden, about 60 to 70 minutes.

Remove the pudding from the roasting pan. Cool on a rack, then chill thoroughly. Let it stand at room temperature about 30 minutes before serving.

Orange Bread Pudding

Makes 8 servings

This is a deliciously rich and custardy bread pudding, generously spiked with orange, developed by my friend Ruth Cousineau. Bread puddings are a time-honored way of using up yesterday's loaf, and deserve a better reputation than they generally have.

Bread for puddings can be in slices, cubes or crumbs; in her American Cookery *(1796), Amelia Simmons calls for soft bread or biscuit, soaked in milk, then "run thro' a sieve or cullender." Half a century later, in her* New Receipts for Cooking *(1852), Miss Eliza Leslie directed her readers to grate stale biscuits, soak and sieve them, and bake them in puddings made in large breakfast cups.*

Mrs. Mary Lincoln, whose Boston Cook Book *(1887) was the forerunner of the 1896* Boston Cooking-School Cook Book *by Fannie Farmer, bakes her bread pudding with "fine stale bread crumbs," and then goes on to offer intriguing variations: "Add one cup of raisins," she advises, "and you have a* Plum Pudding . . . And this becomes the Queen of Puddings *by leaving out the whites, and after baking, spreading a layer of* jam *over the top, then a méringué of the whites and browning slightly."*

Cooking tip: For delicate, creamy results, take care not to overcook this pudding.

12 slices French or Italian bread, sliced about ⅜ inch thick
3 tablespoons unsalted butter, melted
3 eggs
3 egg yolks
½ cup sugar
Pinch salt
Grated zest of 2 oranges
Juice of 1 orange
2 tablespoons Grand Marnier
2⅓ cups milk
1 cup heavy cream

Preheat the oven to 325 degrees. Bring a kettle of water to the boil; set it aside, off the heat.

Brush the slices of bread with melted butter on one side of each; set them, buttered sides up, on a foil-lined sheet pan. Toast the bread in the oven, turning over once, until lightly golden (this can also be done in a broiler, but watch carefully to avoid burning). Set the toasted bread aside.

Whisk together the eggs, yolks, sugar, salt, orange zest, orange juice, Grand Marnier, milk and cream until well blended.

Arrange the toast slices, buttered sides up, in an 8-by-8-inch (or 7-by-11-inch) baking dish, forming neat, overlapping rows. Pour the custard over the toast gently, then place the pan in a larger baking pan lined with several sheets of newspaper. Let the bread absorb the custard for about 15 minutes.

Place the pans in the oven and pour enough hot water into the larger pan to come halfway up the sides of the pudding. Bake until nearly set, but still slightly wobbly in the center, about 30 to 40 minutes. Remove the pudding from its water bath and cool on a wire rack. Serve lukewarm or chilled.

Cabinet Pudding

Makes 8 servings

This cake and custard pudding, spiked with lemon and brandy, is a simplified version of a recipe from Francatelli's Modern Cook, *published in London in 1865. Francatelli lined a decorative mold with dried cherries and candied citron, alternated layers of sponge cake and ratafias or macaroons, and filled the mold with an egg yolk custard similar to the one in this recipe.*

Cabinet pudding was popular in England, where it was sometimes called Chancellor's pudding. It is actually quite similar to a trifle, which is not baked, but assembled in a bowl.

It's interesting to see how recipes change once transported; a virtually identical old French recipe is made with brioche and called pouding de cabinet. *Louis de Gouy, the French chef at New York's Ritz-Carlton (famed as the creator of Vichyssoise), elaborated considerably on the theme. His version included ladyfingers brushed with currant jelly, a gelatinized custard, and chopped angelica, candied apricots, pineapple, red and green cherries, pears and citron.*

⅓ of a Light Sponge Cake
(see page 64)
¼ cup currants or raisins
12 egg yolks
1 cup sugar
3 cups milk
3 tablespoons brandy
Grated zest of 1 lemon

Preheat the oven to 325 degrees. Bring a kettle of water to the boil; set it aside, off the heat.

Using a long serrated knife, slice the cake into layers about ¼ inch thick. Arrange them to cover the bottom of a 7-by-11-inch baking dish, cutting pieces to patch gaps as necessary. Scatter the currants over the cake and set aside.

Whisk together the egg yolks, sugar, milk, brandy and lemon zest in a mixing bowl until blended. Pour the custard over the cake, press the cake gently into the liquid with a spatula, and let the mixture soak in for 5 minutes or so.

Place the dish in a larger baking pan lined with a few sheets of newspaper, and pour in enough hot water to come halfway up the sides of the pudding.

Bake in the preheated oven until the custard has set but is still slightly wobbly in the center (it will set further as it cools), about 50 to 55 minutes. Carefully remove the custard from its water bath and cool on a wire rack. Chill before serving.

Little Tapioca Puddings with Caramel

Makes 6 servings

Some people hate *tapioca; in his* American Cookery, *James Beard recalls jokes about "fish-eye" pudding. In my family, we called tapioca "frogs' eyes," but we all still love it, particularly as a soothing late-night snack. This unmolded version is one of my favorite recipes in this collection, the light creamy custards offset by their caramel glaze. I like them best served warm.*

Cooking tip: *When making caramel, be sure to dissolve the sugar completely before bringing the mixture to a boil.*

CARAMEL:
½ cup sugar
3 tablespoons cold water

⅓ cup quick-cooking tapioca
3 tablespoons sugar
Pinch salt
1½ cups cold milk
2 eggs, separated
2 tablespoons unsalted butter
1 teaspoon pure vanilla extract

Preheat the oven to 325 degrees. Bring a kettle of water to a boil, then remove it from the heat. Set out 6 ½-cup ramekins or custard cups in a shallow baking dish.

To make the caramel, put the sugar and water in a small, heavy-bottomed saucepan and heat over moderate heat. Brush down any sugar crystals from the sides of the pan with a brush dipped in cold water. Be sure that all the sugar has dissolved before the mixture comes to a boil. Boil, uncovered, watching carefully to avoid burning. When the sugar turns a medium amber color, remove the pan from the heat. Immediately pour the caramel into the 6 ramekins, dividing it evenly and swirling it to coat the bottoms. Set aside.

Stir together the tapioca, sugar and salt in another saucepan; gradually stir in the cold milk. Bring the mixture to a boil, stirring constantly with a wooden spoon. Remove the pan from the heat and stir in the egg yolks, butter and vanilla. Set aside, stirring once or twice as it cools slightly.

Beat the egg whites until just stiff but not dry; fold them gently into the tapioca mixture. Gently pour the mixture into the prepared ramekins and place them, in their baking dish, on the center rack of the oven. Pour enough hot water into the dish to come halfway up the sides of the ramekins.

Bake in the preheated oven until set and very pale gold, about 25 minutes. Remove the dish from the oven and allow the puddings to cool 5 to 10 minutes in their water bath. Run a sharp knife around the edges of the puddings and invert each onto a plate. Serve warm. They may also be chilled after unmolding.

Crème Brûlée

A luxuriously rich custard, with a crunchy caramel topping, based on the original recipe for "burnt cream" from Cambridge University. This was traditionally prepared with a salamander, a wooden-handled iron which was heated in a live fire, then passed over the dish. The reflected heat caramelized the sugar topping instantly without overcooking the custard below. Burnt cream was apparently also a favorite of the Jefferson family at Monticello, whose recipe concludes, "sift powdered sugar over it and glaze it with a hot shovel."

Cooking tip: Be sure to chill the custard thoroughly before glazing it, to keep it cool and smooth. Place the cooled crème brûlée *in a pan of ice water before slipping it under the broiler.*

2 cups heavy cream
8 egg yolks
1 teaspoon pure vanilla extract (optional)
⅓ cup (approximately) light brown sugar

Preheat the oven to 325 degrees. Bring a kettle of water to a boil, set it aside, off the heat.

Heat the cream in a heavy-bottomed saucepan until it just comes to a boil; lower the heat, and simmer 45 seconds. Meanwhile, whisk the yolks until smooth. When the cream is ready, whisk it very gradually into the yolks until well blended.

Scrape the mixture back into the saucepan and stir constantly over very low heat until it is thickened enough to coat the back of a spoon. This will take only 2 or 3 minutes; do *not* let the mixture boil. Remove the pan from the heat, stir in the vanilla, if you are using it, and immediately strain into a shallow baking dish.

Set the dish in a larger baking pan lined with several sheets of newspaper and place it in the preheated oven. Pour enough water from the kettle into the larger pan to come halfway up the sides of the custard in its dish.

Bake the custard until nearly set, but still slightly wobbly in the center (a toothpick should emerge not quite clean). This will take only 8 to 10 minutes. Remove the pan from the oven. Remove the dish of custard from its water bath and cool on a wire rack. Chill thoroughly.

Preheat the broiler with the rack about 6 inches from the source of heat. Strain an even ⅛-inch-thick layer of brown sugar over the surface of the custard; smooth the layer with a spatula or the back of a spoon.

Broil the custard until the top has caramelized to a rich brown. Watch almost constantly, because it can burn very quickly. Cool briefly, and serve as soon as possible, cracking the glazed topping with the back of a spoon, and serving some topping and the custard to each person.

Creamy Rice Pudding

Makes 6 to 8 servings

I love all kinds of rice puddings—as long as they're freshly made, and not starchy. Old English and American cook books offer a surprisingly diverse range: Amelia Simmons includes six versions in her American Cookery *(1796), including one made with ground rice. Mrs. Lincoln's rice puddings include hot, cold and souffléed versions (Carême also used ground rice to thicken dessert soufflés), and Miss Leslie has one flavored with bitter almonds or peach kernels.*

I stumbled onto this creamy version when I was testing something quite different, and have been enjoying it ever since.

⅓ cup currants
3 tablespoons brandy (optional)
1 cup long-grain white rice
1½ cups milk
½ cup sugar
Pinch salt

VANILLA CUSTARD SAUCE
(CRÈME ANGLAISE):
2 cups milk
6 egg yolks
⅓ cup sugar
1 teaspoon pure vanilla extract

1 cup heavy cream, whipped until
   not quite stiff

If you are using brandy, soak the currants in it for at least 30 minutes.

Blanch the rice in boiling water for 2 minutes, then drain and rinse under cold water. Bring the milk to a boil with the sugar and salt. Add the rice, stir, and simmer over very low heat, covered, until the rice is quite tender, about 30 to 35 minutes. Transfer to a bowl and cool.

To make the sauce, bring the milk to a boil in a heavy-bottomed saucepan. Meanwhile, whisk the egg yolks and sugar in a mixing bowl until combined. Dribble in the hot milk very gradually, whisking constantly. Return the mixture to the saucepan and stir constantly with a wooden spoon over low heat. After about 6 minutes, the custard will thicken enough to coat the back of a spoon evenly. Do not allow it to boil. Strain it into the rice, stir in the vanilla and the soaked currants, and cool the mixture.

Fold in the whipped cream gently just before serving.

Cornmeal Pudding with Hard Sauce

Makes 8 to 12 servings

This recipe comes from Mrs. Merras Brown, a superb cook who lives in Phoenix. Although she was a professional caterer in Chicago for many years, her home cooking has a decidedly Southern flavor (see page 54).

Cornmeal is, of course, a staple ingredient in American cooking, and was ingeniously used in breads, sauces and even drinks by native American Indians. In 1847, Eliza Leslie wrote The Indian Meal Book: comprising the best receipts for the preparation of that article. *Many recipes for cornmeal puddings (usually called Indian or hasty pudding) call for seven or eight hours' baking time; this firm version takes considerably less. "Eat with sauce," Marion Harland advised in* The New England Cook Book *(1887), "or with cream and sugar. It is very nice."*

¾ cup yellow cornmeal
½ cup molasses
1½ cups boiling milk
1-1½ teaspoons powdered
    ginger, to taste
¼ teaspoon salt
½ cup finely chopped suet (or
    4 tablespoons butter, cut up)
1 egg, lightly beaten
1 cup cold milk

HARD SAUCE:
8 tablespoons (4 ounces) unsalted
    butter
1 cup sugar
¼ cup bourbon, rum or brandy

Preheat the oven to 300 degrees. Butter a 1½-quart casserole or soufflé dish.

Stir together the cornmeal and molasses in a large mixing bowl. Add the boiling milk, ginger and salt, stirring. Stir in the suet or butter and eggs, mixing until smooth. Pour this mixture into the prepared casserole and let it stand for a few minutes without stirring.

Gently pour the cold milk over the top; do not stir it in, as this will form the "jelly." Bake in the preheated oven for 1½ hours.

To make the hard sauce, beat the butter until light and fluffy. Add the sugar gradually, creaming constantly. Add the spirits and mix in well. Chill briefly, then stir again.

Serve the pudding warm with the hard sauce.

Noodle Kugel (JEWISH NOODLE PUDDING)   Makes 8 to 10 servings

No Jewish meal is complete without a noodle pudding, which is frequently too sweet and very heavy. This is a lighter kugel, *based on a recipe of Jennie Grossinger's, by way of my mother. It's usually made with wide egg noodles, but you might like to try it with narrow noodles for textural contrast.*

½ pound egg noodles
1 teaspoon salt
2 eggs
¼ cup sugar
½ teaspoon cinnamon
1 cup coarsely grated apple
½ cup raisins
3 tablespoons unsalted butter,
    melted

TOPPING:
½ cup breadcrumbs, whole wheat
    if available
¼ cup sugar
¾ teaspoon cinnamon
2-3 tablespoons melted butter

Preheat the oven to 350 degrees. Butter an 8- or 9-inch-square baking pan.

Cook the noodles with the salt in a large saucepan of boiling water until just tender; do not overcook. Drain; rinse under cold water and drain again.

Meanwhile, whisk together the eggs, sugar and cinnamon until blended. Stir in the apple, raisins, melted butter and drained noodles until combined. Pour into the prepared baking dish and gently smooth the top.

To make the topping, stir together the breadcrumbs, sugar and cinnamon in a small bowl. Sprinkle this mixture in an even layer over the noodles, then drizzle the surface with melted butter.

Bake in the preheated oven until crisp and golden, about 35 minutes. Serve warm, cut into squares.

Steamed Pumpkin Pudding with Ginger-Lemon Cream

Makes 12 to 16 servings

There's nothing like a steamed pudding to conclude a traditional holiday feast. We are most familiar with plum pudding, which at Christmas is decked with a sprig of holly and set alight. But the range of steamed puddings is much broader than we might suspect; 19th-century cookbooks frequently list dozens of varieties. Most of these were made with generous quantities of suet paste in which a fruit filling was rolled; the pudding was then wrapped in cloth and boiled. A jam roly-poly, prepared this way, is still a popular treat in England.

In her Directions for Cookery *(1848), Miss Leslie notes that "we have known of a very rich plum pudding being mixed in England and sent to America in a covered bowl; it arrived perfectly good after a month's voyage, the season being winter."*

I think you'll appreciate the lightness of this steamed pumpkin pudding and its whipped cream sauce.

⅔ cup dates, coarsely chopped
½ cup currants
2 tablespoons crystallized
   ginger, finely minced, or
   more to taste
⅓ cup brandy
¼ cup rum
1¼ cups soft, fresh breadcrumbs,
   preferably whole wheat
3 eggs
½ cup sugar
¼ cup brown sugar
1 tablespoon molasses
3 cups pumpkin puree, fresh
   (see Note) or canned
½ cup flour
2 teaspoons baking powder
½ teaspoon ground allspice
¼ teaspoon grated nutmeg
¼ teaspoon salt
Pinch ground cloves
3 tablespoons butter, melted

Heavily butter a 1½-quart mold, preferably one with a central tube, such as a kugelhopf or ring mold.

Toss together the dates, currants, crystallized ginger, brandy and rum in a small bowl. Set aside to macerate, tossing occasionally, for at least 1 hour, or overnight.

Strain the liquid from the fruits and ginger into a mixing bowl and stir in the breadcrumbs until moistened. Set aside.

Whip the eggs, sugar and brown sugar in an electric mixer until very fluffy, about 4 minutes. Gently stir in the molasses and the pumpkin puree, then the crumb mixture. Meanwhile, sift the flour, baking powder, allspice, nutmeg, salt and cloves onto a sheet of wax paper. Set aside about 3 tablespoons of this mixture.

Add the flour mixture and melted butter alternately to the pumpkin mixture, adding a little at a time, and folding gently. Quickly toss the reserved fruit with the reserved flour mixture and fold into the pudding batter. Pour into the prepared mold. Place a sheet of buttered foil over the top of the mold, fastening it securely but leaving a little room for expansion.

Set up a steamer: Place a wire rack in a large pot with a tight-fitting lid. Choose a pot large enough to allow steam to circulate around the mold; I often improvise by raising a wire cake rack on a small tart mold, to allow room for a good inch of water. Add hot water to the pot to come up to

GINGER CREAM:
1½-2 cups heavy cream
2 tablespoons crystallized
   ginger, finely minced,
   or to taste
Grated zest of 1 lemon

the level of the rack; bring to a boil. Carefully place the pudding mold on the rack and cover the pot.

Steam for 2 hours, maintaining a steady but gentle boil. You may have to add water to keep the level constant; be careful not to let the water boil away. The timing can vary, and will probably be longer if your mold does not have a central tube. After 2 hours, the pudding should be set but still slightly moist in the center. If a toothpick does not emerge clean, steam the pudding for another 15 minutes, or until done. Remove it from the steamer and take off the foil, laying it loosely over the pudding.

(This pudding can be prepared in advance; simply re-steam the cooled pudding in a covered mold for 30 minutes, or until heated through.)

Unmold onto a platter, decorate if you wish (a sprig of holly is traditional) and serve warm in slices, with ginger cream.

To make the ginger cream, whip the cream until nearly stiff. Stir in the crystallized ginger and lemon zest. Spoon a little cream over each slice of pudding and pass the rest separately.

NOTE: To make fresh pumpkin puree, break off the pumpkin stem, cut the pumpkin in half crosswise, and scoop out the seeds and stringy material. Place the halves, cut side up, on a foil-lined baking sheet and cover and seal each half with foil. Bake in a preheated 350-degree oven until the flesh is very tender, about 1½ hours. Cool slightly. Scoop out the flesh and mash with a potato masher or in the food processor. You may substitute canned unsweetened solid-pack pumpkin puree.

A NOTE ON CHOCOLATE

In the entire realm of desserts, nothing arouses passion like chocolate. Some fancy imported chocolates are currently retailing for up to $80 per pound, and books on chocolate desserts seem to fly out of the stores.

Brought to Europe from Mexico by the late 16th century, chocolate was considered a potent aphrodisiac in the Spanish court. Recently, research has indicated that there may be a valid scientific reason for chocolate's allure. It seems that two doctors discovered that cocoa beans contain a substance called phenylethylamine (derived from phenylalanine, an amino acid), which is also the chemical produced by the brain when we fall in love.

Writers quickly embraced this theory, even going so far as to claim that a craving for chocolate was actually a chemical response to loneliness (which didn't surprise me, given some of the chocolate addictions I have encountered).

A chocolate expert assures me, however, that while the beloved bean does indeed contain this "love chemical," about ten times the amount can be found in a single hamburger, and that there's plenty in a glass of milk.

For whatever reason, the passion for chocolate is at an all-time high, so I've included a special soufflé and a simple sauce in this collection. Both are designed to satiate the most fervent chocolate addict.

Chocolate Soufflé The Quilted Giraffe   *Makes 6 servings*

A chocolate soufflé is not exactly old-fashioned home-cooked fare (and isn't, strictly speaking, a pudding), but this recipe, by Barry Wine and Mark Chayette of New York's superb restaurant, The Quilted Giraffe, is so good that I couldn't resist including it here.

Mr. Wine prefers Callebaut bittersweet chocolate from Belgium; if you can't get that, use a top-quality Swiss chocolate. He also frequently transforms the soufflés into a "Mocha Fantasy" by dropping a small scoop of coffee ice cream into the center of each soufflé as it emerges from the oven.

Cooking tip: *Leave the soufflés slightly liquid in the center, and serve them immediately.*

9 ounces top-quality bittersweet chocolate, cut up
12 tablespoons (6 ounces) unsalted butter
6 egg yolks
1 tablespoon water
14 egg whites
2 tablespoons sugar
1¼ cups heavy cream, whipped

Preheat the oven to 400 degrees. Butter 6 1¼-cup soufflé dishes or ramekins; coat the insides with sugar, shaking the excess sugar from each dish into the next one.

Melt the chocolate with the butter over hot water. Meanwhile, beat the egg yolks and water in an electric mixer with the whisk attachment until very light, about 5 minutes. Gently fold the chocolate mixture into the beaten yolks.

Whip the egg whites just until stiff and glossy, but not dry; add the sugar during the last 10 seconds of beating.

Fold about a quarter of the whites into the chocolate mixture. Fold in the remaining whites gently but thoroughly. Fill the prepared dishes with the batter, smoothing the tops gently. Run your thumb around the edge of each soufflé, forming a groove in the batter.

Place the soufflés on a baking sheet and bake in the preheated oven until browned but still soft in the center, about 12 minutes. Serve immediately, spooning some of the whipped cream into the center of each soufflé, and passing the remaining cream separately.

Brandy Chocolate Sauce
Makes about 2 cups

Having gone on about the joys of homemade desserts, it's now time to admit that on many busy nights, there's just no time to make one. Still, it is nice to treat yourself to something at the end of the meal. Fresh fruit will do, and there are few things as soothing as good ice cream.

But when you want to make it a little more special, try keeping a dessert sauce on hand. A puree of fresh or frozen berries can make a plain piece of cake, scoop of sherbet or bowl of fruit memorable, and a good vanilla custard sauce (see page 36) can help nearly anything.

This chocolate sauce, however, is guaranteed. In the days when I used to run a restaurant, many guests would overlook more "elegant" desserts and insist on a big dish of ice cream with our brandy chocolate sauce and sliced toasted almonds. We prepared the sauce in huge batches, but the demand always kept us running out sooner than expected. With chocolate, too much is never enough.

Cooking tip: If you don't have brewed coffee on hand, substitute ¼ cup cream and 1 teaspoon instant espresso powder. Or if you prefer not to use the coffee flavoring, simply substitute with ¼ cup cream.

4 ounces best-quality semisweet chocolate, cut up
2 ounces unsweetened chocolate, cut up
4 tablespoons unsalted butter, cut up
⅓ cup sugar, or to taste
¾ cup heavy cream
¼ cup strongly brewed coffee
2-3 tablespoons Cognac, or Armagnac
1 teaspoon pure vanilla extract

Place the chocolate, half of the butter, the sugar, cream and coffee in a small, heavy-bottomed saucepan over direct but moderate heat.

Stirring gently with a wooden spoon, bring the mixture to a boil. Boil very gently for about 4 minutes, stirring. Add the brandy and simmer for about 2 more minutes, stirring. If desired, correct the seasoning with a little more sugar or brandy, simmering the sauce for another minute or so.

Remove the pan from the heat and stir in the rest of the butter and vanilla, stirring until the sauce is completely smooth. Serve warm. Reheat leftover sauce gently in a water bath or double boiler.

When a neighbor appears at a farmer's home at mealtime, and is, of course, invited to eat, he can get out of it by saying: "Thanks, I just got up from the table." After that the most a housewife can press on him is a cup of coffee or a glass of buttermilk. Unless there is pie. A man can always accept a piece of pie. On the farm, pie is the great common denominator.

— RACHEL PEDEN,
Speak to the Earth

Pies
&
Tarts

Two-Layer Lemon Pie

Like the popular lemon sponge pudding, this pie separates into cake and custard layers as it bakes. Lemon tarts were popular in Devonshire centuries ago, and according to Farm Journal, *lemon pie is one of the best-loved American pies (along with apple, cherry and pumpkin).*

While lemon meringue pie is very nearly a national institution, there are several other traditional lemon pies. These include the Shaker lemon pie, with two crusts surrounding paper-thin lemon slices with rind, lemon chiffon pie, open-face French-style tarts, and Grant's lemon pie, a double-crust affair with a curd filling that contains raisins and coconut.

½ recipe Basic Pie Pastry
  (see page 82)
3 tablespoons unsalted
  butter, softened
1 cup sugar
Grated zest of 3 lemons
¼ cup plus 2 tablespoons
  fresh lemon juice
3 eggs, separated
6 tablespoons sifted flour
1⅓ cups milk

Preheat the oven to 400 degrees.

Roll out the pastry to fit a deep 9½- or 10-inch pie dish. Transfer the pastry to the dish, fitting it in loosely, cutting off any excess, and forming a crimped border, if you like. Line the pastry shell with foil, fill with rice or beans, and bake 5 minutes, or until the sides have set. Remove the foil and weights, and bake until faintly golden, about 6 minutes more. If bubbles rise, prick the crust lightly with a fork. Remove the pastry from the oven, and lower the heat to 350 degrees. Allow the crust to cool slightly.

Cream the butter and sugar in a mixing bowl until fluffy. Beat in the lemon zest and juice, then the egg yolks, blending well. Stir in the flour, then the milk, stirring until smooth.

Beat the egg whites until they are stiff but not dry; fold them gently into the filling. Place the crust on a baking sheet, place on the oven rack, and carefully pour in the filling. Bake at 350 degrees until set and lightly browned, about 35 to 45 minutes. Cool the pie before serving.

Country Peach Pie

The simplest and best peach pie, bursting with juice and the fresh flavor of summer's ripe fruit.

1 recipe Basic Pie Pastry
   (see page 82)
6 large ripe peaches
1 tablespoon lemon juice
⅓ cup brown sugar
¼ cup granulated sugar
2 tablespoons cornstarch
Pinch each cinnamon, mace (or
   nutmeg) and salt
2 tablespoons chilled butter,
   cut into bits

GLAZE:
1 tablespoon milk
1 tablespoon sugar

Preheat the oven to 425 degrees, with a rack in the lower third of the oven.

Roll out slightly more than half the pastry on a lightly floured surface to a large circle ⅛ inch thick (or less) and carefully transfer it to a deep 9½- or 10-inch pie dish. Roll the remaining pastry to a large circle and transfer it to a foil-lined baking sheet. Chill the pastry.

Dip the peaches in boiling water for about 15 seconds, then peel off their skins. Place the lemon juice in a large mixing bowl. Working quickly, stone and slice the peaches thickly, letting them fall into the bowl. You should have about 6 cups. Toss gently and discard any excess juice.

Sift together the brown and white sugars, cornstarch, cinnamon, mace and salt. Toss gently with the peaches, then pour the mixture into the pastry-lined pie plate, mounding the peaches slightly in the center. Dot with butter. Moisten the edge of the crust with cold water, then lay the top crust over loosely. Trim off excess pastry, leaving a ¾-inch overhang. Turn the edges under the pastry, forming a smooth border on the rim of the pie plate. Crimp the border.

Brush the pastry lightly with milk, then sprinkle with sugar for a light glaze. Cut several slashes in the top crust to release steam, and place the pie on the foil-lined baking sheet. Cover the border of the pastry with strips of foil if you like, to prevent overbrowning.

Bake in the preheated oven until golden brown, 40 to 45 minutes, removing the strips of foil after 20 minutes.

Cool the pie on a wire rack. Serve warm or at room temperature, preferably with vanilla ice cream.

Double-Berry Lattice Pie

Makes 8 servings

Berries of the bramble,
How I love to ramble
Through the shady valleys,
And pluck you as I go!
—From "BLACKBERRIES" by CHARLES MACKAY

A classic American berry pie, not too sweet, and with slightly runny juices.
    Cooking tips: Mix the cornstarch thoroughly with the dry ingredients first to prevent lumps.
Covering the pie briefly with foil will help melt the sugar and heat the berries through.

**1 recipe Basic Pie Pastry
    (see page 82)**
**4½-5 cups (2 boxes)
    blackberries and blueberries,
    picked over**
1 tablespoon fresh lemon juice
**¾-1 cup sugar (depending on
    sweetness of berries;
    I usually use the lesser
    amount)**
3 tablespoons cornstarch
Pinch cinnamon
**1 tablespoon cold butter,
    cut into bits**
**1 tablespoon milk or cream,
    for glaze**
1 tablespoon sugar, for glaze

Vanilla ice cream

Preheat the oven to 425 degrees.

Roll out a little more than half the pastry to a large circle ⅛ inch thick and carefully transfer it to a 9½- or 10-inch pie dish. Trim the edge, leaving a ½-inch overhang. Roll the remaining pastry to a circle to fit the dish and transfer it to a foil-lined baking sheet. Chill the pastry.

Toss the berries with the lemon juice in a large bowl. Stir together the sugar, cornstarch and cinnamon in a separate bowl, using a fork. Quickly but thoroughly toss this dry mixture with the berries.

Pour the berry filling into the bottom pastry crust and dot with the butter pieces. Moisten the edge of the crust with cold water. Cut the separate circle of pastry into 1-inch-wide strips, using a rippled pastry cutter or a sharp knife. Lay half the strips across the top of the pie at even intervals, pressing them into the edges of the bottom crust. Lay the remaining strips of pastry across the top, placing them at an angle and pressing them into the edge of the pastry. Trim off the ends of the strips, then fold the overhanging edge of the bottom crust over onto the rim of the pie plate, pressing gently to form an even rim. Form a decorative border, if you like. Glaze the pastry by brushing with the milk, then sprinkling with sugar.

Place the pie on a baking sheet, preferably one made of black steel. Cover loosely with foil and bake in the preheated oven for 12 minutes. Remove the foil and bake until the pastry is golden brown and the filling is bubbly, about 45 to 50 minutes total.

Cool the pie before serving with vanilla ice cream.

The Coach House Pecan Pie

Makes 8 servings

An important Southern dessert tradition, pecan pies were made with the ingredients found in the winter larder: sugar, molasses, eggs, and the glorious pecans grown in Georgia and other Southern states. Pecan pie was reputedly a favorite dessert of Abraham Lincoln.

This recipe comes from Leon Lianides, whose Greenwich Village restaurant, The Coach House, serves some of the finest American food in this country.

Cooking tip: *You might want to arrange some additional pecan halves over the surface of the pie before baking.*

1 recipe Rich Pastry (below), or use Basic Pie Pastry (page 82)
3 eggs
1 cup light corn syrup
1 cup plus 1 tablespoon dark brown sugar
2 tablespoons melted butter
½ teaspoon pure vanilla extract
½ teaspoon cinnamon
Pinch salt
1 cup whole fancy pecans (or more, if using to decorate pie surface)
Whipped cream or ice cream

Preheat the oven to 400 degrees.

Roll out the pastry and use it to line a 10-inch pie plate, forming a decorative border if you like. Chill the pastry.

Whisk the eggs lightly in a mixing bowl until combined. Add the corn syrup, sugar, butter, vanilla, cinnamon and salt, and whisk until smooth. Stir in the pecans.

Pour the mixture into the pie shell. If you like, arrange more pecans over the surface of the filling. Place the pie on a baking sheet (preferably a heavy black one) and bake in the preheated oven for 15 minutes.

Lower the oven heat to 350 degrees and continue to bake until the filling is almost set in the center, about 30 to 35 minutes longer. Remove the pie from the oven and cool on a rack. Serve at room temperature with whipped cream or ice cream.

THE COACH HOUSE RICH PASTRY

1½ cups sifted flour
Pinch salt
8 tablespoons (4 ounces) unsalted butter, softened
1 egg yolk
2 tablespoons ice water

Place the flour and salt in a mixing bowl. Make a well in the center; add the butter, egg yolk and ice water to the well. Mix the ingredients with your fingers until they are homogeneous and the dough is cohesive. Form into a ball, wrap in plastic and chill at least 45 minutes before rolling out.

Butterscotch Cream Pie

Makes 8 servings

A smooth version of another American favorite. This recipe was given to me by Nancy Hubbard, a fine home cook in Indiana. This is a treasured recipe from Nancy's mother, who used to prepare it years ago as a special treat for Nancy and her brother Mike. Both still enjoy it today, and I think you will, too.

GRAHAM CRACKER CRUST:
⅓ pound graham crackers, crushed or processed into crumbs (about 1¼-1½ cups crumbs)
2 tablespoons sugar
6 tablespoons melted butter

FILLING:
¾ cup dark brown sugar
⅓ cup cornstarch
Pinch salt
3 cups milk
4 egg yolks
1 teaspoon pure vanilla extract
2 tablespoons unsalted butter

TOPPING:
½-⅔ cup heavy cream
1 tablespoon confectioners' sugar
¼ teaspoon pure vanilla extract

Preheat the oven to 350 degrees. Butter a 10-inch pie plate.

Combine the graham cracker crumbs, sugar and butter; press into the pie plate evenly. Bake 10 minutes in the preheated oven; allow the crust to cool thoroughly.

To make the filling, stir together ½ cup of the brown sugar, the cornstarch and salt in a mixing bowl. Stir in about 3 tablespoons of the milk and set aside. Bring the remaining milk, brown sugar and the salt to a boil in a saucepan.

Meanwhile, add the egg yolks to the mixing bowl and whisk until completely smooth. When the milk is boiling, add a splash of milk to the mixing bowl, whisking well (this heats the yolks slowly, preventing curdling). Repeat the process 2 or 3 times, then scrape the mixture back into the saucepan and bring to a boil, stirring constantly with a wooden spoon. Be sure to stir around the inside bottom rim of the pot. Boil, stirring, for 2 minutes, then strain the custard into a clean mixing bowl. Whisk in the vanilla and butter until smooth; then place a sheet of plastic wrap on the surface of the custard and let cool. When cool, pour the custard into the crust; top with wax paper, and chill.

To make the topping, whip the cream and sugar until stiff; stir in the vanilla. Pipe a double border around the edge of the pie, using a pastry bag with a large star tip. If you prefer, the whipped cream can simply be spooned onto each slice when serving.

Edna Lewis's Raspberry Pie

Best known as the author of A Taste of Country Cooking, *Edna Lewis was raised in Freetown, Virginia, a farming community of freed slaves. She is a superb cook and a delightful woman, with great dignity and humor. Her raspberry pie resembles an elegant jewel box, with the red berries glistening through the cut-out pastry lid. Feel free to increase the quantity of raspberries if your budget allows.*

1 recipe Lard Pastry (below),
   or ½ recipe Basic Pie Pastry
   (page 82)
1½ pints fresh raspberries
3 tablespoons sugar
1 tablespoon cornstarch, or
   more as needed
Whipped cream

Preheat the oven to 375 degrees.

Roll out the pastry on a lightly floured surface until quite thin; carefully transfer it to an 8- or 9-inch pie plate. Trim off the edges, reserving them. Press the tines of a fork into the edges of the pastry to form an attractive border.

Gently gather up the pastry trimmings and roll them out into a circle about ⅛ inch thick. Lay a plate about 5 inches in diameter over the pastry and trim off the edges, forming a neat circle. Use a star-shaped cookie cutter to cut out the center of the circle, then use a sharp knife to cut a zig-zag pattern around the outside edge. Carefully transfer the circle of pastry to a baking sheet lined with foil. Line the pastry crust in the pie plate with foil also, then weight it down with beans or rice.

Place both the baking sheet and the pie dish in the pre-heated oven. Bake the lower crust until set but not colored, about 8 minutes. Remove the foil and beans carefully, and continue baking until the crust is light gold and baked through, about 12 to 14 minutes longer. Meanwhile, bake the smaller circle of pastry until lightly browned, about 13 minutes ("Watch it like a *hawk,*" warns Edna Lewis). When each portion is done, carefully remove it to a rack to cool.

Lower the oven heat to 350 degrees. Place the raspberries in a shallow baking dish, sprinkle with the sugar, and bake until they get soft and begin to bleed their juice, but are still whole. (This usually takes 8 to 10 minutes.) Remove the dish from the oven and cool on a rack.

Holding the raspberries back with a slotted spoon, pour the raspberry juice into a small saucepan. Stir in the cornstarch, then bring the mixture to a boil and cook gently for 10 minutes. (If the liquid has not thickened, add a little more cornstarch, dissolving it in cold water first.) Remove the glaze from the heat. When it has cooled slightly, use your finger to brush about a tablespoon of the glaze over the bottom crust. Carefully arrange the berries over the crust, reserving about 2 tablespoons for later. Spoon the glaze over the berries (reserving a little), then gently lay the disk of pastry over the center of the pie. Fill the center of the disk with the reserved berries, then brush them with the reserved glaze.

Serve with whipped cream.

EDNA LEWIS'S LARD PASTRY

1 cup flour
¼ teaspoon salt
⅓ cup chilled lard
Cold water as needed

Use a pastry blender to cut together the flour, salt and lard. Sprinkle with cold water, adding just enough to allow the pastry to pull together. (It should not be sticky). Make into a ball and chill.

Italian Rice and Ricotta Pie

Makes 8 servings

This recipe, a light interpretation of the Italian torta di riso, *was adapted from one given to me by Mrs. Mary Codola, a warm, generous woman whose idea of a snack is a superb five-course meal. A native of Rhode Island, she still prepares delectable Italian dishes as her mother, mother-in-law and grandmother did—including the lightest pasta I've ever eaten. This pie is equally good warm or cold, and is a good choice for a picnic.*

½ recipe Cookie Crust
   (see page 83)
¾ cup long-grain rice
Boiling water
¾ cup plus 2 tablespoons
   milk
Scant ½ cup sugar
Pinch salt
1 cup (about 8 ounces) ricotta
   cheese, pressed through a sieve
1 egg
1 egg yolk
¾ teaspoon pure vanilla
   extract
½ cup heavy cream
Pinch cinnamon

Preheat the oven to 350 degrees.

Roll out the pastry and fit it in a deep 9½-inch pie dish. Set aside.

Cook the rice in boiling water, uncovered, for 5 minutes. Drain; rinse under cold water and drain again. Bring the ¾ cup milk, ¼ cup of the sugar and salt to a boil in a heavy saucepan. Stir in the rice, and simmer, partially covered, until it is nearly, but not quite, tender (test carefully; timing can vary).

Meanwhile, combine the sieved ricotta, 2 tablespoons milk, the remaining sugar, egg, egg yolk and vanilla in a mixing bowl, stirring until smooth. Slowly stir in the rice mixture.

Whip the cream until it forms soft peaks; fold into the mixture in bowl. Pour the filling into the pastry shell and sprinkle the surface lightly with cinnamon.

Place the pie on a heavy baking sheet and bake until golden and set in the center, nearly 1 hour. Cool on a wire rack. Serve at room temperature or chilled.

Pumpkin Soufflé Pie

What moistens the lip, and what brightens the eye,
What calls back the past, like the rich pumpkin pie?
—From "THE PUMPKIN," by JOHN GREENLEAF WHITTIER

As much as turkey and cranberry sauce, pumpkin pie means Thanksgiving. The pumpkin is native to the New World, and was much used in native American Indian cooking. There is, however, an old English recipe in which the pumpkin is sliced and fried with herbs and spices, then baked in pastry with apples and currants. This went out of fashion in the 18th century, so pumpkin pie has come to be an exclusively American preserve (when I baked a pumpkin pie for co-workers in London, they were baffled).

Eighteenth-century American recipes for pumpkin and other custard pies are usually referred to as "puddings"; Amelia Simmons offers two for "pompkin pudding." Both are surprisingly similar to the pies we enjoy today.

In American Cookery, *James Beard notes that Yankees preferred pies made of squash or pumpkin, whereas Southerners preferred a similar pie, made with sweet potatoes (see page 54). Also, he points out that spices were not included in the pies until trade ships made them a more common commodity.*

2 cups pumpkin puree, fresh (see page 39) or canned (unsweetened)
3 tablespoons maple syrup
¼ cup dark brown sugar
¼ cup granulated sugar
1 tablespoon flour
½ teaspoon salt
½ teaspoon cinnamon
¼ teaspoon ground allspice
¼ teaspoon nutmeg
Pinch freshly ground pepper
4 eggs, separated
½ cup heavy cream
½ cup milk
3 tablespoons rum or Bourbon
1 teaspoon pure vanilla extract
Unbaked deep 9½-inch pie shell, made with ½ recipe Basic Pie Pastry (see page 82)
Whipped cream

Preheat the oven to 425 degrees, with a rack at the center level.

In a mixing bowl, whisk together the pumpkin puree, maple syrup, sugars, flour, salt and spices. Whisk in the egg yolks, cream, milk, rum or Bourbon, and vanilla until smooth.

Beat the egg whites until stiff but not dry. Fold about a quarter of the egg whites into the pumpkin mixture; then gently fold in the rest.

Place the pastry-lined pie dish on a baking sheet (preferably a heavy black one) and pour in the filling. Bake in the preheated oven for 10 minutes; then lower the heat to 375 degrees and bake about 45 minutes longer, until the filling has puffed and is set in the center. Cool before serving, preferably accompanied by whipped cream.

Sweet Potato Pie with Almond Crunch Topping

Makes 8 servings

Another winning recipe from Mrs. Merras Brown, this pie has an irresistible crunchy topping that contrasts with its smooth custard filling. "My mother always told me I was a natural-born cook," says Mrs. Brown. "From the age of five, I started to cook on my own little stove that actually worked." With her "invaluable inheritance of cooking knowledge" from her parents and grandparents (with influences of Black, Indian, French, Irish and South American cooking), Mrs. Brown went on to become a professional cook of remarkable talent and enthusiasm.

Sweet potatoes were enjoyed by the American Indians, and in the hands of Southern black cooks, they became an important contribution to American cooking. Early Southern recipes for sweet potato pie, flavored with lemon rind, nutmeg and brandy, were called "puddings." However, Fannie Farmer, who offers over two dozen pie recipes, makes no mention of sweet potato pie. We Northerners don't know what we've been missing!

1 recipe Flake Pie Dough (below) or ½ recipe Basic Pie Pastry (see page 82)

FILLING:
2 cups mashed sweet potatoes (see Note)
¾ cup brown sugar
½ cup granulated sugar
2 tablespoons maple syrup
1 teaspoon cinnamon
½ teaspoon nutmeg
¼ teaspoon allspice
½ teaspoon salt
¾ cup milk or cream
¼ cup Bourbon or dark rum
2 eggs, lightly beaten
2 tablespoons butter, melted

ALMOND CRUNCH TOPPING:
¼ cup brown sugar
¼ cup flour
2 tablespoons butter
½ teaspoon nutmeg
⅓ cup coarsely chopped almonds
Whipped cream

Preheat the oven to 400 degrees.

Roll out the pastry to fit a deep 9½-inch pie plate. Crimp the edges and set aside.

Beat the sweet potatoes briefly in an electric mixer until fluffy, then add the sugars, maple syrup, cinnamon, nutmeg, allspice and salt. Beat in the milk, Bourbon, eggs and butter until smooth. Pour the filling into the pie shell and bake in the preheated oven just until set, about 40 minutes.

Meanwhile, rub together the brown sugar, flour, butter and nutmeg until coarsely crumbled. Add the almonds and toss together briefly.

Scatter the topping over the pie, lower the oven heat to 375 degrees, and return the pie to the oven. Bake 15 minutes longer. Cool before serving with plenty of whipped cream.

NOTE: To make 2 cups mashed sweet potatoes, peel and cut up 1¼ pounds sweet potatoes and cook in boiling water 15 to 20 minutes, until tender. Drain well, and mash, or press through a strainer, until smooth. (Steaming the sweet potatoes, or baking them whole, takes a little longer, but results in an even better texture.)

MRS. BROWN'S FLAKE PIE DOUGH

2 cups flour
½ cup plus 2 tablespoons
   chilled butter
½ cup chilled lard
½ teaspoon salt
Ice water

Sift the flour, baking powder and salt into a mixing bowl. With a pastry blender or 2 knives, cut in the ½ cups butter and lard until coarsely crumbled. Add the ice water a little at a time and mix with a fork until the dough is moist enough to hold together. Form the dough into a ball, wrap and chill thoroughly.

Roll out the dough on a lightly floured board, dot with the remaining 2 tablespoons butter, then roll up the dough like a jelly roll and chill it again before rolling out.

Hungarian Cheese Tart
Makes 8 to 10 servings

I have never been a fancier of cheesecake as a dinner dessert (too heavy), but this tart is something else again. Based on a recipe of the late Hungarian chef Károly Gundel, its airy vanilla-scented cheese filling is reminiscent of a homemade cheese strudel. Try to enjoy it warm.

Deep 9½-inch pie
   shell, made with ½ recipe
   Cookie Crust or 1 recipe
   Sweet Tart Pastry (see page
   83) partially baked
   (see page 57)
1 pound cottage cheese,
   pressed through a sieve
¾ cup heavy cream
4 egg yolks
½ cup plus 2 tablespoons
   sugar
Grated zest of 1 lemon
½ teaspoon pure vanilla
   extract
6 egg whites
½ cup golden raisins
1 tablespoon flour

Preheat the oven to 350 degrees.

Combine the sieved cottage cheese, cream, egg yolks, ½ cup sugar, lemon zest and vanilla in a large mixing bowl until blended.

Beat the egg whites until they form soft peaks; gradually add the 2 tablespoons sugar and continue beating until stiff but not dry. Stir a large spoonful of the whites into the cottage cheese mixture to lighten it; then fold in the rest until nearly combined.

Quickly toss the raisins with the flour and add to the cheese mixture; fold gently just until combined. Pour the filling into the pastry shell.

Bake in the preheated oven until golden and set in the center, about 45 minutes. Serve warm or at room temperature.

Prune Mirliton with Grand Marnier
(A NUT CAKE FROM NORMANDY)

Makes 10 to 12 servings

This outrageously rich layered confection is a variation on a traditional recipe from Normandy, where mirlitons *are usually baked as miniature tartlets, flavored with macaroons or ground almonds and apricot jam.*

**1 recipe Sweet Tart Pastry
   or ½ recipe Cookie Crust
   (see page 83)**

BOTTOM LAYER:
⅓ cup (generous) hazelnuts
**1 cup (about 7 ounces)
   prunes, chopped**
⅓ cup honey
⅓ cup Grand Marnier
Grated rind of ½ orange

TOP LAYER:
**1½ cups ground almonds
   (about 6 ounces; grind in
   a food processor along
   with the sugar below)**
⅔ cup sugar
4 eggs, lightly beaten
**4 tablespoons unsalted butter,
   melted, cooked until pale-
   medium brown, and cooled
   slightly**

GLAZE:
1 egg yolk
2 teaspoons Grand Marnier

Preheat the oven to 350 degrees, with a rack about one-third of the way up from the bottom.

Butter an 8- or 9-inch cake pan; roll out the pastry and fit it into the pan. Chill.

To make the bottom layer of the mirliton, toast the hazelnuts in a small pan in the preheated oven until they begin to color slightly, about 10 minutes. Chop coarsely. Stir nuts together with the prunes, honey, Grand Marnier and orange rind in a mixing bowl. Set aside.

Prepare the top layer by stirring together the almonds, sugar, eggs and browned butter in a mixing bowl, or food processor.

To assemble the mirliton, trim the edges of the pastry flush with the rim of the pan. Pour in the prune mixture for the bottom layer, smoothing it to form an even layer. Pour the almond mixture over to form the top layer, smoothing it evenly. Bake in the lower third of the preheated oven until set, about 45 minutes. Remove from the oven for glazing.

Make the glaze by stirring together the egg yolk and liqueur and gently brush an even layer over the surface of the cake. Return to the oven and bake 5 minutes longer.

Cool the cake completely before serving. Serve cut in wedges.

Ruth's Rustic Autumn Tart

Makes 8 servings

A chunky fruit-and-nut tart. Pears can be substituted for the apples; you might like to try pecans instead of walnuts. And a dab of crème fraîche or ice cream is welcome, especially if you serve the tart warm.

1 recipe Sweet Tart Pastry (see page 83)

3 tart apples (e.g., Granny Smiths), peeled, cored and cut roughly into ½-inch chunks

1 cup pitted prunes, halved or quartered

1 cup walnuts, roughly broken in coarse pieces

½ cup sugar

6 tablespoons (3 ounces) unsalted butter, melted

3 egg whites, beaten once or twice with a fork

Preheat the oven to 400 degrees.

Line a 10-inch quiche pan with pastry, forming a high border. Chill, if you have time. Line the crust with foil; weight down with rice or beans. Place on a heavy baking sheet and bake in the preheated oven until the edges are set, 5 to 6 minutes. Remove the foil and weights, return to the oven and bake until very faintly colored, another 6 minutes or so. Prick with a fork any bubbles that puff up as the pastry bakes. Remove the pastry shell from the oven and lower the heat to 375 degrees.

Meanwhile, in a large mixing bowl, combine the apples, prunes, walnuts, sugar, melted butter and egg whites, tossing with your hands until the ingredients are combined and lightly coated.

Pour this mixture into the pastry shell and cover lightly with foil. Bake for 30 minutes at 375 degrees, then remove the foil and continue to bake until the apples are tender and the filling is lightly browned, about 30 minutes longer. If you like, sprinkle with a little more sugar (or confectioners' sugar) for the last 10 minutes of baking time. Cool on a wire rack, then serve warm.

Alsatian Apple Tart with Macaroon Crunch Topping

In Alsace, rustic tarts are made with all the fruits that have lent their names to the region's famed eaux-de-vie: poires, mirabelles, quetsches and myrtilles *(pears, yellow and purple plums, and huckleberries, respectively). Combining fruits with custard is a regional tradition; the delicate, crunchy topping is a variation I learned from Chef Bernard at the Cordon Bleu.*

Cooking tip: *Be careful not to overcook the apples; McIntosh add plenty of flavor, but can quickly turn to mush.*

**1 recipe Sweet Tart Pastry
(see page 83)**
**3 McIntosh apples, peeled,
quartered, cored and cut in
¼-inch slices**

CUSTARD:
2 eggs
1 egg yolk
3 tablespoons sugar
**½ cup heavy cream
or crème fraîche (page 84)**
¼ cup milk
½ teaspoon pure vanilla extract

MACAROON TOPPING:
**¾ cup thinly sliced almonds
(about 3 ounces)**
¼ cup sugar
3 tablespoons currants
1 egg white

Preheat the oven to 400 degrees.

Line a 9- to 10-inch quiche pan with pastry, forming a high border. Chill, if you have time. Line the crust with foil; weight down with rice or beans. Place on a black baking sheet, if you have one. Bake in the preheated oven until the edges are set, 5 to 6 minutes. Then remove the foil and weights and bake until very faintly colored, another 6 minutes or so. Prick with a fork any bubbles that puff up. Lower heat to 350 degrees.

Arrange the apple slices in the shell, overlapping them slightly, in a circular pattern. Fill in the center with the remaining apple slices. Bake the tart, still on the baking sheet, until the apples just begin to get tender, about 12 minutes. Do not overcook the apples, because they will cook further.

To make the custard, whisk together the eggs, egg yolk, sugar, cream, milk and vanilla. Pour the mixture carefully over the apples, nearly up to the level of the edge of the pastry. Bake until the custard is just set in the center, 20 to 23 minutes. Remove the tart from the oven.

To make the macaroon topping, stir together the almonds, sugar, egg white and currants. The mixture should be very lightly coated with egg white. If it is too dry, stir in a few drops more egg white. Carefully spoon the topping onto the surface of the tart, smoothing gently with a palette knife or the back of a spoon. Return the tart to the oven and bake until lightly golden, about 15 to 20 minutes.

Cool the tart before serving slightly warm or at room temperature.

Galette Bressane
(GEORGES BLANC'S CRÈME FRAÎCHE TART)

Makes 8 servings

This recipe, originally made with brioche dough, comes from Chez La Mère Blanc, the esteemed restaurant in the Bresse region of France, where Georges Blanc became the youngest chef ever to be awarded three Michelin stars. This rustic country dessert is a specialty of Georges's grandmother, the original "Mère" Blanc.

Cooking tip: Try to use crème fraîche (page 84) rather than heavy cream, for especially mellow flavor.

⅓-½ recipe Sour Cream
   Kuchen Dough (see page 70)
Flour as needed
¾ cup crème fraîche
   or heavy cream
3 tablespoons sugar
½ teaspoon pure vanilla extract
1 tablespoon softened butter
1 egg yolk
1 tablespoon water

Butter an 11-inch porcelain quiche pan or other shallow baking dish, or a baking sheet. Prepare the yeast dough as directed, allowing it to rise until doubled. Punch the dough down and knead it on a lightly floured board, adding enough flour (about ½ cup) to form a somewhat firmer dough. Roll out the dough into a 12-inch circle and press it into the bottom and sides of the baking dish or pan. Cover with oiled plastic wrap and set aside until the dough is puffy, about 30 minutes.

Whip the cream until fluffy; add 1 tablespoon of the sugar and the vanilla and whisk until soft peaks form. Set aside.

Preheat the oven to 375 degrees.

With the back of a fork press down the dough on the bottom of the pan. With your finger press the dough firmly into the sides of the pan, pushing up a rim around the top. Spread the soft butter over the bottom.

Beat the egg yolk with the water and brush the glaze over the outer rim of dough. Use a rubber spatula to spread the whipped cream evenly over the bottom, then sprinkle the cream with the remaining 2 tablespoons of sugar.

Bake in the preheated oven 12 to 15 minutes, or until the cream has browned lightly and the dough has baked through. Serve warm.

Caramel Walnut Tart

Think of this tart as a sort of lightened pecan pie, but with the caramel and the slightly bitter walnuts providing a sharp edge to the sweet cream filling. This is one of my favorites.

9- or 9½-inch tart
   shell, made with 1 recipe
   Sweet Tart Pastry (see page
   83), partially baked
   (see page 59)
⅔ cup sugar
¼ cup cold water
1¼ cups heavy cream
1 teaspoon pure vanilla extract
1 tablespoon unsalted butter
2 eggs, lightly beaten
3 tablespoons sugar
1½ cups walnuts, coarsely
   chopped, plus 10 walnut
   halves
Unsweetened whipped cream

Preheat the oven to 400 degrees. Prepare the pie shell.

Make a caramel by stirring together the sugar and water in a small, heavy saucepan over moderate heat. Use a brush dipped in cold water to wipe down any sugar crystals from the sides of the pan. Be sure the sugar has dissolved completely before the mixture comes to the boil. Boil the mixture, without stirring, until it turns medium amber; watch carefully to avoid burning.

Remove the pan from the heat and carefully add the cream; the mixture will sputter violently. Return the pan to the heat and stir to dissolve the caramel. Boil gently, stirring, until lightly thickened, 7 to 8 minutes. Remove the pan from the heat and stir in the vanilla and the butter.

Whisk the eggs and sugar in a bowl until blended, then gradually whisk in the caramel mixture. Stir in the chopped walnuts and pour the mixture into the prepared pie shell. Arrange the walnut halves decoratively around the edge of the tart. Place the tart on a baking sheet and bake in the preheated oven until set, but still slightly wobbly in the center, about 20 minutes. (A toothpick inserted near the center will not emerge quite clean.) Cool the tart on a wire rack before serving slightly warm or at room temperature, with unsweetened whipped cream.

*There is no one department in cooking
where so much depends upon the baking
as in making cake.*

—Mrs. Lincoln's Boston Cook Book, 1887

*Wastefulness is to be avoided in every
thing; but it is utterly impossible that
cakes can be good (or indeed any thing
else) without a liberal allowance of good
materials. Cakes are frequently rendered
hard, heavy, and uneatable by a
misplaced economy in eggs and butter;
or tasteless and insipid for want of their
due seasoning of spice, lemon &c.*

—ELIZA LESLIE, Directions for
Cookery in its Various Branches, 1848

---

*B*ecause early ovens were not reliable, home-baked cakes are a relatively recent development. By the early 20th century, however, housewives were satisfying the American sweet tooth with all sorts of cakes and cookies, and the bake sale became a favorite form of fund-raising (and socializing).

Where did this lead? Unfortunately, to the packaged cake mix, whose popularity has, I hope, peaked. We are now rediscovering the pleasures of baking cakes from scratch, using the freshest ingredients we can find.

Cakes
&
Cookies

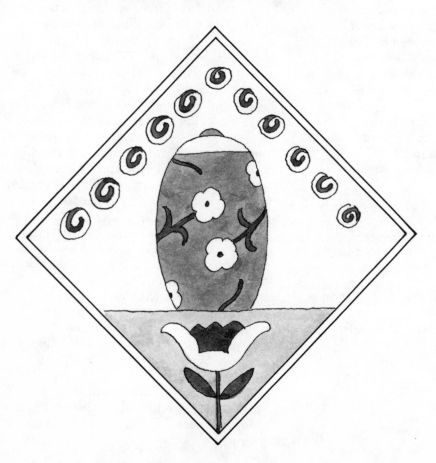

Peach-Pecan Upside-Down Cake

Makes about 8 servings

We have all had too many commercial versions of the American favorite, upside-down cake, usually made with sticky-sweet canned pineapple and cherries. Traditionally, upside-down cakes were baked in a cast-iron skillet, and when made with a light sponge cake and fresh fruit, there's no reason why they can't be very good indeed. If fresh peaches and pecans are not available, feel free to substitute sliced ripe pears and walnuts. I tested this several times before concluding that beating the whole eggs and sugar gives results just as voluminous as when the eggs are separated and the whites beaten separately.

8 tablespoons (4 ounces)
  unsalted butter
¾-1 cup brown sugar, lightly
  packed (use the greater amount
  if the peaches are tart)
3 medium-size peaches (about
  1 pound), peeled by being
  dipped briefly into boiling
  water, then skinned
½-⅔ cup pecan halves

LIGHT SPONGE CAKE:
¾ cup all-purpose flour
¼ cup cornstarch
1 teaspoon baking powder
Pinch salt
4 large eggs
¾ cup sugar
Grated zest of 1 small
  lemon
½ teaspoon pure vanilla extract

1 tablespoon rum or Bourbon
  (optional)
Whipped cream (optional)

Preheat the oven to 350 degrees.

Place the butter in a 9-inch-square cake pan, a 10-inch ovenproof skillet, or a 9½- to 10-inch pie plate. Put the pan in the oven while the oven is preheating until the butter has melted. Remove the pan from the oven and reserve 1 tablespoon of the melted butter in a small cup.

Pour the brown sugar over the melted butter in an even layer. Halve the peaches, discard the stones and slice them ½ inch thick. Arrange the slices in neat rows over the brown sugar. Arrange the pecan halves in rows, fitting them into all the empty spaces. Set the pan aside.

To make the sponge cake, sift together the flour, cornstarch, baking powder and salt, and set aside. Using an electric mixer, beat the eggs, sugar and lemon zest until very thick, pale yellow and at least doubled in volume, about 5 minutes. Turn off the mixer and fold in the vanilla and the reserved tablespoon of melted butter until nearly blended. Working quickly, fold in the dry ingredients, adding about ¼ cup at a time, and using a light touch. When the ingredients are thoroughly blended together, pour the batter into the prepared cake pan and place in the preheated oven.

Bake until the cake is puffed, lightly golden, and the center springs back when pressed lightly, about 35 minutes. Remove the cake from the oven, run a small sharp knife carefully around its edges, and immediately invert it onto a serving plate. Leave the pan on top of the cake.

After a few minutes, carefully remove the pan, and sprinkle the peaches very lightly with the rum, if you are using it. Serve warm or at room temperature with whipped cream.

Chocolate Almond Cake

Makes 8 to 10 servings

This easy, flourless cake, with a texture reminiscent of a dense fudge brownie, is loosely adapted from a torte recipe developed by the late Helen McCully, the influential food editor of McCall's *and* House Beautiful. *It takes only minutes to make, and people always seem to want the recipe.*

8 tablespoons (4 ounces)
  unsalted butter, softened,
  plus more for the pan
4 ounces semisweet chocolate
½ cup sugar
1 tablespoon apricot preserves
1 tablespoon Grand Marnier
3 eggs
1 cup blanched almonds, ground
  finely in a food processor

Grated zest of 1 orange
¼ cup dry breadcrumbs
Confectioners' sugar
Vanilla Custard Sauce
  (see page 36) or whipped cream

Preheat the oven to 375 degrees. Butter the sides of an 8-inch round cake pan. Line the bottom of the pan with parchment or wax paper. Butter the paper lightly, and set the pan aside.

Melt the semisweet chocolate in a small saucepan over low heat; allow to cool slightly.

Cream the 8 tablespoons butter with the sugar in a small bowl until well blended and light. Add the preserves, Grand Marnier and 1 egg, beating constantly. Add the remaining eggs, one at a time, beating constantly. Stir in the chocolate, ground almonds, orange zest and breadcrumbs. Pour the mixture into the prepared pan.

Bake in the preheated oven for 25 minutes. (Do not overbake; the cake should be slightly moist in the center.) Cool the cake in its pan on a wire rack. Turn it out of the pan onto the rack and remove the parchment.

Sprinkle the cake with confectioners' sugar. Serve in wedges, surrounded by a thin pool of custard sauce, or with whipped cream.

Ligita's Latvian Apple Cake

Makes 8 servings

This excellent, easy recipe was given to me by Karolyn Nelke, a playwright friend who loves to cook. It's almost like a quick apple pie without the crust. I found that letting the butter brown slightly adds a mellow flavor, but it isn't necessary.

3 medium-size apples (I usually use Granny Smiths), peeled, quartered, cored and sliced

1 teaspoon lemon juice

2 tablespoons plus ¾ cup sugar, plus more as needed

2 teaspoons cinnamon

12 tablespoons (6 ounces) unsalted butter, cut up

1 cup sifted flour

1 egg, lightly beaten

Preheat the oven to 350 degrees. Generously butter a 10-inch pie pan.

Toss the apple slices in a bowl with the lemon juice, 2 tablespoons sugar and cinnamon. Spread the apples evenly in a pie pan.

Melt the butter over moderate heat; let it cook until lightly golden. Watch carefully—it should take about 7 minutes. Pour the butter into a bowl, leaving behind any sediment in the pan. Add ¾ cup sugar to the butter, stirring. Gently stir the flour and egg into the mixture until blended. Spread this batter evenly over the apples and sprinkle with about a tablespoon of sugar.

Bake in the preheated oven until lightly golden and crusty, 40 to 45 minutes. Cool the cake on a rack. Cut in wedges and serve warm or at room temperature; I like it with vanilla ice cream.

Ginger Cake

Pound cakes, another English tradition, appear in nearly all the classic books on American cookery. Ginger cake, a variation on the theme, was a staple with tea, and in many households there was always one in the pantry, carefully stored in an airtight tin. This is a simple and delicious cake which freezes well, and, baked in small foil loaf pans (for slightly less time than indicated below—test carefully), makes a welcome holiday gift.

The preserved ginger adds the best flavor, but crystallized ginger can be substituted. If you aren't crazy about ginger, use about ½ cup white raisins, currants, or chopped dates instead.

16 tablespoons (½ pound) unsalted butter, softened
1 cup sugar
1¾ cups flour
½ teaspoon baking powder
¼ teaspoon salt
5 eggs
1 teaspoon pure vanilla extract
2 tablespoons freshly squeezed orange juice
3 tablespoons preserved ginger (in syrup), drained and minced
1 teaspoon syrup from the preserved ginger

Preheat the oven to 325 degrees. Butter and flour a 4½-by-8½-inch loaf pan and set aside.

Beat the butter in an electric mixer until creamy, then add the sugar and cream and beat until the mixture is light and fluffy, for at least 5 minutes (don't rush this step).

Meanwhile, sift the flour, baking powder and salt onto a sheet of wax paper. Lower the mixer speed and gradually add this dry mixture to the creamed mixture. When it is not quite blended in, add the eggs one at a time, mixing until the batter is smooth before each addition. Add the vanilla, orange juice, ginger and syrup; mix just until the batter is smooth.

Pour the batter into the prepared pan and bake on the center rack of the preheated oven until it is golden and tests done (a toothpick should emerge dry from the center of the cake). This should take about 1 hour and 15 minutes, but test carefully, as the timing may vary. If the cake begins to brown before it has baked through, cover the top loosely with foil.

Cool the cake on a wire rack for 15 minutes, then remove it from the pan. After a few minutes longer, lay a clean kitchen towel over the top.

When it has cooled completely, wrap the cake in a plastic bag. Allow to ripen overnight before slicing with a serrated knife.

NOTE: This cake also toasts nicely (especially when it begins to get stale).

Rich Gingerbread

Makes 8 servings

The history of gingerbread can probably be traced farther back than that of any other baked item except bread. Those who are interested should consult Karen Hess's commentary in Martha Washington's Book of Cookery, *published by Columbia University Press in 1981. I'll just mention that recipes for medieval spiced cakes made with breadcrumbs go back at least as far as the 13th century, and that pepper, which I've included here, was usually included with the spices.*

The popularity of gingerbread in Colonial America—18th- and 19th-century cookbooks frequently give recipes for no fewer than a dozen varieties, including snaps, drops and other cookies—reflects the growing trade in West Indian molasses and Jamaican ginger, and also the keeping qualities of this dense cake. I'm quite pleased with this moist version, which is based on Eliza Acton's recipe. Serve it with the chunky applesauce below, or with whipped cream, or with a lightly thickened lemon sauce.

2 eggs
¾ cup molasses
1 scant cup dark brown sugar, lightly packed
4-5 teaspoons ground ginger
Pinch each allspice, cinnamon and freshly ground black pepper
Grated zest of 1 lemon
2 cups sifted flour
6 tablespoons butter, melted
½ cup buttermilk
¼ cup milk
1 teaspoon baking soda

Preheat the oven to 350 degrees. Butter and flour an 8-inch-square cake pan.

Beat the eggs in an electric mixer until light and frothy. Add the molasses and continue beating. Stir together the brown sugar, ginger, allspice, cinnamon, black pepper and lemon zest and gradually add this mixture to the eggs until blended.

Lower the mixer speed slightly. Beating constantly, add about a third of the flour, then the butter, then another third of the flour. Quickly stir together the buttermilk, milk and baking soda and add this to the batter, mixing gently. Add the remaining flour, mixing just until blended evenly. Pour the batter into the prepared cake pan.

Bake in the preheated oven until the gingerbread has shrunk slightly from the sides of the pan and a toothpick inserted in the center emerges clean, about 45 minutes. Do not overbake.

Cool on a wire rack, then cut in large squares and serve directly from the pan, with the applesauce below or whipped cream.

CHUNKY APPLESAUCE

Makes a generous 1½ cups

4 tart apples, e.g. Granny
   Smiths, peeled, cored and cut
   in ¾-inch dice
Juice of 1 lemon
½ cup sugar, or less to taste

Toss together the apples, lemon juice and sugar in a heavy saucepan. Cover and cook over moderate heat, stirring occasionally, until the apples start to give off their juices. As the apples soften, mash some of them lightly. They should be cooked—a tender puree with large chunks still intact—after 12 to 15 minutes. If there is still a layer of liquid in the pan, continue to cook, uncovered, until slightly thickened.

Transfer the applesauce to a bowl and cool. Add a drop or two of lemon juice, if needed.

Rich Soft Spice Cake

Makes an 8-inch-square cake

Another simple but outstanding recipe from Karolyn Nelke, this cake, with its distinctive scent of cardamom, is from her Finnish great-aunt.

2 eggs
1¾ cups brown sugar
8 tablespoons (4 ounces)
   unsalted butter, melted
   and cooled
2 cups sifted flour
2 teaspoons cinnamon
1 teaspoon ground cardamom
1 teaspoon baking powder
½ teaspoon baking soda
¼ teaspoon salt
1 cup sour cream
Confectioners' sugar, for
   decorating

Preheat the oven to 350 degrees. Butter an 8-inch-square cake pan, then coat with fine breadcrumbs or flour, shaking out any excess. Set the pan aside.

Beat the eggs with the sugar with an electric mixer or whisk, until very light and fluffy, about 5 minutes. Stir in the cooled butter just until blended.

Meanwhile, sift together onto a sheet of wax paper the flour, cinnamon, cardamom, baking powder, baking soda and salt. Add the sifted dry ingredients, alternating with sour cream, to the egg mixture. When the batter is smooth, turn it into the prepared pan.

Bake in the preheated oven until the cake has set in the center (a toothpick should emerge clean), about 40 to 50 minutes. Cool it completely on a wire rack, then sift on a light layer of confectioners' sugar and cut into squares.

Sour Cream Kuchen with Two Toppings

Makes 2 9-inch cakes

American housewives have always been fond of coffee cakes. Books like The Joy of Cooking *(my own favorite cookbook) and* The Settlement Cook Book *offer many yeast cakes which reflect the influence of German and Scandinavian immigrants in the Midwest. This is a light, buttery cake, delicious with morning coffee, afternoon tea or brunch.*

KUCHEN DOUGH

2 packages dry yeast
¼ cup lukewarm water
12 tablespoons (6 ounces) unsalted butter
¾ cup sugar
2 eggs
2 egg yolks
½ teaspoon salt
1 teaspoon pure vanilla extract
½ cup lukewarm milk
½ cup sour cream
3¾ cups flour, or more if needed
2 tablespoons melted butter

Combine the yeast and lukewarm water in a small cup and set aside.

Cream the butter and sugar in an electric mixer until light and fluffy. Add the eggs, one at a time, then the egg yolks. Add the salt, vanilla, milk, sour cream and yeast mixture, beating until smooth.

If your mixer has a dough hook, switch to it now. Add the flour; the dough will be very soft and sticky. It should not, however, be a liquid batter; add a bit more flour if necessary. It will not be firm enough to come away from the sides of the bowl. Knead until very silky and elastic, 8 to 10 minutes. Place the dough in a buttered bowl, turn over to coat, and cover with a damp towel. Set aside in a warm place until doubled in volume (the dough can also rise overnight, refrigerated).

Punch the dough down and divide in half. Each of the topping recipes is for one-half of the dough; if you do not want to make both at once, the remaining dough can be refrigerated or frozen until needed. (These cakes also freeze well fully baked.)

Preheat the oven to 375 degrees. Butter a 9-inch-square cake pan (or a 10-inch round baking dish).

Pat the dough evenly into the pan and brush with 1 tablespoon melted butter. Let rise until nearly doubled. Gently spread on one of the toppings below and bake until golden brown, about 30 to 35 minutes. Cool the kuchen thoroughly on a wire rack before cutting it into squares.

PLUM STREUSEL TOPPING

For a 9-inch cake

1 pound plums (5-6), stoned
   and thickly sliced
Sugar, if needed
½ cup flour
⅓ cup brown sugar
¼ teaspoon cinnamon
3 tablespoons chilled butter
3 tablespoons chopped almonds

If the plums are very tart, toss them with a little sugar.

Cut together the flour, brown sugar, cinnamon and butter until crumbly. Stir in the chopped almonds.

When the cake has risen in its pan, arrange the plum slices in even rows over the surface. Sprinkle the streusel mixture over in an even layer and bake as directed.

BIENENSTICH (BEE-STING) GLAZE

For a 9-inch cake

This was a specialty of a bakery in my hometown, where the cake was baked with this bee-sting glaze, then split and filled with a vanilla pastry cream. I have prepared it here without a filling, because I find it rich enough as it is.

⅓ cup (generous) brown sugar
3 tablespoons heavy cream
3 tablespoons unsalted butter
3 tablespoons honey
Few drops fresh lemon juice
⅔ cup almonds with their skins,
   coarsely chopped, or ⅔ cup
   sliced blanched almonds

Stir together the brown sugar, cream, butter and honey in a small, heavy saucepan. Bring to a boil and boil 30 seconds. Remove the pan from the heat and stir in the lemon juice and almonds.

When the cake has risen in its pan, pour this topping evenly over the surface and bake as directed.

Buttermilk Shortcake

Another all-American farm tradition, old-fashioned shortcakes were little more than an excuse to devour great quantities of juicy summer berries with fresh cream. I know enough not to get involved in the bitter biscuit-vs.-sponge cake shortcake controversy; let's just I say I find this rich New England-style biscuit dough irresistible when drenched with ripe berries or peaches.

I have always liked this type of shortcake, and was inspired by a Cuisine *cover photograph of a raspberry version made by Helen Witty. See the Note below for a lighter sponge-cake version. Researching shortcakes, Associated Press food editor Cecily Brownstone has found yet a third version: a Southern recipe made with pastry dough. And an intriguing Southern variation on the theme finds creamed chicken served between layers of hot cornbread.*

2 cups flour
⅓ cup plus 1 tablespoon sugar
½ teaspoon salt
1 teaspoon baking powder
½ teaspoon baking soda
6 tablespoons unsalted butter, chilled
1 egg yolk
⅔ cup buttermilk (approximately), or as needed

3-4 cups berries; sugar; whipped cream

Preheat the oven to 400 degrees. Butter an 8-inch round cake pan.

Sift the flour, ⅓ cup sugar, salt, baking powder and baking soda into a mixing bowl. If you are using a food processor, simply pulse the dry ingredients on and off twice. Cut in the butter until the mixture is crumbly. Put the egg yolk in a 1-cup measure and add enough buttermilk to measure ⅔ cup. Stir to blend, then add enough of the liquid to the flour mixture to form a soft, moist dough (it usually can take the full ⅔ cup). Stir very gently with a fork to blend; do not over-work. Gather the dough together gently, scraping the sides of the bowl.

With lightly floured fingertips, pat the dough lightly into the buttered pan, forming an even round. Sprinkle with the remaining tablespoon of sugar. Bake in the pre-heated oven until golden, about 25 minutes. Cool the shortcake briefly on a wire rack, then very carefully remove it from the pan. Use a serrated knife to split it into 2 layers—be careful; this shortcake crumbles easily.

Prepare the berries by sprinkling them with sugar (the amount will depend on their ripeness and your individual taste), crushing them lightly, and leaving them to macerate for an hour or two until juicy. Fill the bottom layer of the shortcake with the fruit, replace the top layer and decorate with whipped cream and more whole berries.

NOTE: For a delicious shortcake made with sponge cake, prepare the Light Sponge Cake (page 64) in a 9-inch-square cake pan or a 10-inch pie dish. Cool the cake thoroughly before splitting it into 2 layers.

Chocolate-Flecked Angel Food Cake

Makes 10 to 12 servings

This is the sort of cake that was popular at late 19th-century teas and ice cream socials. Before the days of electric mixers, the whites were beaten by hand with a clean switch, a wire whisk, a three-pronged fork or any of a number of patent rotary gadgets. Mrs. Merras Brown recalls that, when baking cakes like this one, her grandmother "never used a mixer. She would put her egg whites in a huge platter and beat them with a fork until stiff. She had very large hands with short nails which she would scrub as if she were going in to do surgery."

1½ ounces semisweet chocolate
1 cup cake flour, sifted before measuring
1⅓ cups sugar, preferably superfine
½ teaspoon salt
1½ cups egg whites, at room temperature (about 12 large)
1 teaspoon cream of tartar
1 tablespoon fresh lemon juice
1 teaspoon cold water
1½ teaspoons pure vanilla extract
Few drops almond extract (optional)

Preheat the oven to 350 degrees. Cut a sheet of parchment or wax paper to fit the bottom of a 10-inch tube pan, preferably one with a removable bottom and with "legs" for hanging while cooling. Lay the paper in the pan and set aside.

Grate the chocolate finely onto a sheet of wax paper and place in the refrigerator until needed.

Sift together the flour, ½ cup of the sugar and the salt onto a sheet of wax paper. Sift the remaining cup of sugar onto another sheet of paper and set aside. Now sift the flour mixture 3 or 4 more times, sifting back and forth between 2 sheets of paper. This helps to aerate the dry ingredients.

Beat the egg whites with an electric mixer, starting at medium-slow speed. When the whites become foamy, add the cream of tartar, lemon juice, water, vanilla and optional almond extract. Increase the speed and beat continuously until the whites just form stiff peaks, but are not dry.

Lower the speed and beat the sugar into the whites, about 2 tablespoonsful at a time. Beat a little longer until the peaks are stiff but not dry.

Sift about a quarter of the flour mixture into the egg whites and fold it in gently with a large rubber spatula. Repeat 3 more times; do not overmix.

Gently fold the chocolate into the mixture and lightly pour the batter into the prepared pan. Run a knife through the mixture to eliminate any air pockets, then smooth the top with a spatula.

Bake in the preheated oven until the top is lightly golden and the cake springs back when pressed lightly, about 45 minutes.

Remove the cake from the oven and invert it, still in the pan, either on the pan's supporting "legs," or on a narrow-necked bottle. Let the cake "hang" until completely cool.

Run a sharp knife around the edges of the pan and unmold the cake. To serve, break apart with two forks, a cake divider, or untraditionally, use a knife with a serrated edge.

Semolina Cake with Apples

Makes 8 servings

This is a French family recipe from Claude Dionot in Normandy. Semolina is the meal ground from hard durum wheat; it can be found in specialty shops or Italian markets. Though semolina is not as gritty as cornmeal, this cake somewhat resembles the Rhode Island johnnycake, which may have originated as an Indian cornmeal griddle cake. This cake couldn't be easier to prepare; if you like, serve it drizzled with pure maple syrup.

2 cups milk
¼ cup sugar
Pinch salt
⅔ cup semolina
2 small apples, peeled, cored and thinly sliced (about 2 cups)
1 egg, lightly beaten
1 teaspoon pure vanilla extract

Preheat the oven to 400 degrees. Thickly butter an 8-inch round cake pan.

Bring the milk, sugar and salt to a boil in a heavy-bottomed saucepan. Gradually stir in the semolina and boil 5 to 6 minutes, stirring constantly with a wooden spoon, until the mixture is thick and has lost its "raw" taste. Remove from the heat and set aside, stirring once or twice.

Working quickly, prepare the apples and arrange them, overlapping, in concentric circles in the prepared cake pan. If there are some slices left over, scatter them over without disturbing the concentric circles.

Give the semolina mixture a vigorous stir, then beat in the egg and the vanilla. Carefully pour the batter over the apples and bake in the preheated oven until set in the center and lightly golden, about 30 to 35 minutes.

Cool in the pan on a wire rack for a few minutes, then turn out onto a serving plate and serve warm.

Jewish Honey Cake (LEKACH)

This dark loaf, moister than most Jewish honey cakes, is based on a recipe given to me by Lee Ann Fisher, an accomplished home cook and baker. I was recently given a jar of buckwheat honey for use in this recipe; if you can find it, it will produce an even darker cake with a deep earthy flavor.

½ cup raisins
⅓ cup (approximately) orange juice
¾ cup plus 2 tablespoons strongly brewed coffee (or the same amount of hot water mixed with 2 teaspoons instant coffee)
2 tablespoons whiskey, brandy or rum
2 cups plus 2 tablespoons flour
1 tablespoon cocoa
1 teaspoon baking soda
1 teaspoon baking powder
Pinch salt
2 eggs
¾ cup sugar
¾ cup honey
½ cup plus 1 tablespoon vegetable oil
Grated zest of 1 orange
½ cup coarsely chopped walnuts, lightly toasted

Preheat the oven to 350 degrees. Oil or butter a 5-by-9-inch loaf pan. Lay a piece of foil or parchment in the pan to cover the bottom and long sides with a slight overhang. Grease the foil.

Cover the raisins in orange juice; set aside to soak. Stir together the coffee and whiskey; set aside. Sift together the flour, cocoa, baking soda, baking powder and salt onto a sheet of wax paper. Set aside.

Beat the eggs and sugar in an electric mixer until foamy. Beat in the honey, then the oil and orange zest, then the liquid mixture.

Drain the raisins, discarding the juice. Toss the raisins with the walnuts and about ½ cup of the dry ingredients; set aside.

Lower the mixer speed and gradually add the dry ingredients, then the raisin-nut mixture. Do not overmix. Pour the batter into the prepared pan and bake in the preheated oven until the sides of the cake begin to shrink from the pan and a toothpick inserted in the center just emerges clean. This will take 45 to 60 minutes. Do not overbake; this cake should be moist.

Cool briefly in the pan on a wire rack. Run a knife along the ends of the cake, remove it from the pan, peel off the foil and cool thoroughly, top side up.

NOTE: This cake keeps well, tightly wrapped.

Périgord Pumpkin-Rice Cake

This is adapted (and lightened) from an old farm recipe from Périgord, the region in southwest France which is famous for truffles and foie gras. *Traditionally, the cake was baked until golden in an open hearth.*

2 cups milk
⅔ cup sugar
Pinch salt
Grated zest of 1 orange
2 tablespoons orange juice
½ cup long-grain rice
2 cups pumpkin puree
   (see page 39)
3 eggs
¼ cup sifted flour
Whipped cream (optional)

Preheat the oven to 350 degrees. Butter a 1½-quart soufflé dish or a 5-by-9-inch loaf pan. Line the bottom of the baking dish with a piece of parchment or wax paper cut to fit; butter the paper.

Bring the milk, ⅓ cup of the sugar, the salt, orange zest and juice to a boil in a heavy saucepan. Stir in the rice and simmer, covered, until the rice is quite tender, about 30 minutes (the milk will not all be absorbed). Remove from the heat and stir in the pumpkin puree.

Whisk the eggs with the remaining ⅓ cup sugar until they are thick and form a ribbon when dropped from the whisk. Add about a third of the egg mixture at a time to the pumpkin mixture, folding delicately. Gently fold in the flour and pour the batter into the baking dish, smoothing the top.

Bake in the preheated oven until lightly golden and set in the center; a toothpick should emerge clean after 1 hour to 1 hour and 10 minutes (the timing can vary). Cool the cake on a wire rack, then unmold it onto a serving platter. Peel off the paper and serve warm or cold, with whipped cream, if you like.

Crisp Macadamia Wafers

Makes about 4 dozen

In developing this recipe, I tried to bring out the elusive taste of the nuts themselves, without any conflicting flavors. The flavor, I admit, is still pretty difficult to define, but you won't have any problem eating plenty of these fragile, buttery cookies. They are perfect as after-dinner-party petit-fours. Try to eat them soon after baking; if they lose crispness, return them to a 300-degree oven for a few minutes.

Cooking tip: Because these cookies are soft when they emerge from the oven, they can be rolled into tuiles *(curved "tiles") if you like; just drape them over a rolling pin. You must work fairly quickly, because if the cookies become too cool and firm, they will crack when you try to curve them. If this happens, just return the pan of baked cookies to the oven for a minute or two, until warm.*

.Actually, one of the best ways to make tuiles *is to lay the cookies in the French bread pans that have several curved troughs—this way, you can curve a whole sheet of cookies all at once, in seconds.*

16 tablespoons (8 ounces) unsalted butter, at room temperature
½ cup sugar
2 egg whites
½ teaspoon pure vanilla extract
½ cup (about 2 ounces) ground toasted macadamia nuts
½ cup flour, or as needed
½ cup (approximately) toasted macadamia nuts, chopped coarsely

Preheat the oven to 350 degrees. Either use teflon sheet pans for this recipe, or butter and flour several sheet pans.

Cream the butter until light, then add the sugar and beat until very fluffy. Add the egg whites and vanilla.

Measure the ground macadamia nuts in a 1-cup measure, then add enough flour to measure 1 level cup. Stir this mixture into the butter mixture gently; do not overmix.

Drop the batter in teaspoonfuls onto the prepared cookie sheets, spacing them at least 2 inches apart (these cookies spread during baking). Flatten the cookies slightly with the back of a spoon dipped in cold water. Sprinkle each cookie generously with chopped nuts.

Bake in the preheated oven until the edges are golden, 8 to 10 minutes. Cool the cookies for a few minutes on the sheet before gently lifting them to a wire rack to cool. Repeat the process with the remaining batter.

Rich Macaroon Squares

Makes 60 squares

Pastries and macaroons made with ground almonds probably originated in the Middle East and were brought to France by skilled Italian pastry chefs. Marzipan creations had a place of honor on 15th- and 16th-century banquet tables. These almond and hazelnut macaroons, served in tiny squares as an after-dinner sweetmeat, have a crunchy topping with a soft interior. Ruth Cousineau suggested adding the bitter chocolate layer to cut through the sweetness of the macaroon.

Cooking tips: *Take care not to overbake the pastry in the first stage, as it will be baked again. Adding the sugar to the nuts while grinding will prevent them from releasing their oils.*

**1 recipe Cookie Crust
(see page 83)**
2 ounces unsweetened chocolate, melted

MACAROON TOPPING:
2⅔ cups almonds, with their skins (about 11 ounces)
⅔ cup hazelnuts, with their skins (about 3 ounces)
3 cups sugar
2 teaspoons pure vanilla extract
½ teaspoon almond extract
10 egg whites (a generous ¾ cup)

Preheat the oven to 400 degrees.

Roll out the dough slightly larger than a buttered 10½-by-15½-by-1-inch baking pan. Transfer the dough to the pan, allowing the edges to hang slightly over the sides. Chill briefly.

Trim the edges of the dough flush with the pan; prick the dough with a fork. Bake in the preheated oven until lightly golden, about 16 minutes, pricking any bubbles with a fork as they rise. Remove the pan from the oven and brush the pastry with a thin layer of melted chocolate; cool slightly.

To make the macaroon topping, grind the almonds, hazelnuts and sugar in a food processor until finely powdered but not oily; work in batches if necessary. Add the extracts and egg whites, blending until the mixture forms a smooth paste.

Gently spread the topping over the chocolate-topped pastry. (Take care not to let the topping blend with the chocolate, which should remain a separate layer beneath the macaroon.) Smooth the surface with a spatula and bake until lightly browned and crisp, 30 to 35 minutes. Cool the pan on a wire rack.

When cool, use a sharp knife and a ruler to cut the macaroons into ¾- to 1-inch squares. Treat yourself to the crisp edges as you cut. These cookies are best enjoyed the day they are baked, but can be stored in an airtight container with sheets of wax paper between the layers.

CAKES & COOKIES / **79**

Hermits

A soft, spicy version of this favorite American bar cookie, based on a recipe from my Rhode Island friend Mary Codola (see page 52). Hermits keep well, stored in an airtight container.

16 tablespoons (½ pound) unsalted butter, at room temperature
2¼ cups dark brown sugar
3 eggs (plus 1 more, for glazing)
⅓ cup molasses
4 cups flour
1½ teaspoons baking soda
1½ teaspoons cinnamon
1 teaspoon ground cloves
1 teaspoon nutmeg
½ teaspoon salt
¾ cup chopped walnuts
¾ cup (generous) raisins

Preheat the oven to 375 degrees. Line 2 or 3 baking sheets with parchment paper, or butter and flour the sheets, shaking off any excess flour.

Cream the butter until light; then add the sugar gradually, beating until fluffy. Add 3 eggs, one at a time; then add the molasses.

Meanwhile, sift the flour with the baking soda, spices and salt and add to the creamed mixture, beating gently just until incorporated. (Do not overmix.) Stir in the walnuts and raisins.

Form the dough into cylindrical shapes about 2 inches wide, spacing two "logs" per sheet (they will spread when baked). Brush the dough shapes lightly with beaten egg to glaze them.

Bake in the preheated oven until medium brown but still soft; this will take about 12 minutes. In fact, hermits can bake in as little as 10 minutes, or they may take as long as 15. So watch carefully, and do not overbake.

Cool on a rack and bake any remaining dough. When cooled to lukewarm, use a sharp chef's knife to cut cookies 2 inches wide.

Quaresemali Biscuits

This final recipe, for a crunchy Italian nut biscuit similar to the Jewish mandel brot, *represents the final stage in a long adventure. For years, I have loved these cookies, but only in the version I buy at a large Italian market in New York City. The problem was that I could not find out what bakery supplied my market. When I finally discovered that the secret source was Veniero Bakery, I then tried for weeks to get the recipe from the owner. Finally, Joe Fighera, the baker responsible for these crisp biscuits, sat me down and explained how to bake them.*

Because I had to cut down a professional formula which included 35 pounds of almonds, this took a bit of testing. But it was well worth it—and I didn't mind eating several dozen cookies along the way.

Cooking tips: *An excellent variation can be made using half almonds, half hazelnuts. Pastry flour is softer than all-purpose flour; I have also tested this recipe using all-purpose flour, with perfectly acceptable results. Carbonate of ammonia, or hirschhorn, is hard to find these days (see Note), but produces crisp baked goods. (Quaresemali should be "like glass," says Joe Fighera.)*

1 pound whole almonds, with their skins on

2 cups (scant) sugar

2 cups plus 2 tablespoons pastry flour (see Note)

¼ teaspoon ground cinnamon

½ teaspoon carbonate of ammonia (see Note)

5 drops cinnamon oil (see Note)

2 tablespoons plus 1 teaspoon soft unsalted butter

4½ fluid ounces beaten eggs (a little less than 3 large eggs)

Preheat the oven to 375 degrees. Toast the almonds on a baking sheet until lightly colored, about 10 to 12 minutes. Transfer the almonds to the bowl of an electric mixer. Raise the oven heat to 425 degrees.

Add the sugar, flour, cinnamon and carbonate of ammonia to the almonds. Begin to mix slowly, until the ingredients are combined. Add the cinnamon oil and butter and mix until blended.

Add the eggs and mix until the mixture comes together in a cohesive, slightly sticky dough, and the nuts break up slightly.

Butter a piece of parchment or wax paper and place it on a baking sheet. Take about a third of the mixture and form it into a long cylindrical shape, the length of the baking sheet and about 1 inch thick. Flatten the dough slightly with your fingers; it should be no higher than ½ inch and about 2 inches wide. Repeat the process with the remaining dough (you will probably need 2 baking sheets). Brush the dough shapes lightly with a little beaten egg (I usually have some left over after measuring 4½ fluid ounces) thinned with a few drops of water.

Bake in the preheated oven at 425 degrees until the biscuits are an even medium-gold and slightly firm, about 15 minutes; do not let the edges burn (if they are getting too dark before the centers are set, lower the heat to 375 or 400).

Cool the pan briefly on a rack. When the biscuits are still quite warm, slice crosswise with a chef's knife, using a sharp downward motion. The biscuits should be a little less than 1 inch wide. They will become crisp when cool.

These will keep well, but don't keep the container airtight.

NOTE: If you cannot find the pastry flour, carbonate of ammonia and cinnamon oil from local sources, they are available by mail order from H. Roth & Sons, 1577 First Avenue, New York, NY 10028 (212-734-1111).

Basic Preparations

Basic Pie Pastry

Makes 2 9- or 10-inch shells

This basic recipe will never fail you. I have called for it specifically in many recipes, but it can be used in any situation where you want a crisp pie crust. For a savory crust, omit the sugar.

2¼ cups flour
½ teaspoon salt
2 teaspoons sugar
10 tablespoons (5 ounces) cold
 unsalted butter, cut up
3 tablespoons cold solid
 vegetable shortening,
 cut up
¼ cup cold water, or more
 as needed

By Hand:
Sift together the flour, salt and sugar into a large bowl.

Cut the butter and shortening into small pieces over the bowl, letting the pieces fall into the dry ingredients. Rub the mixture together with your fingertips, a pastry blender or 2 knives, until it resembles coarse crumbs; do not overmix.

Sprinkle the cold water over the flour mixture, tossing with a fork all the while. Add more water if necessary, still tossing with the fork, until the pastry can be gently gathered together into a ball. Do not make the dough too wet. Knead the ball once or twice in the bowl to distribute the butter evenly. Gather together into a ball again. Cut in 2 portions; flatten each, wrap and chill at least 1 hour.

With Food Processor:
Add the flour, salt and sugar to the food processor bowl and mix with several on/off pulses.

Add large chunks of butter and shortening to the bowl. Process, using on/off pulses, until the mixture resembles coarse meal; do not overprocess.

Scrape the mixture into a bowl. Add water as directed above and proceed with recipe.

Sweet Tart Pastry

I usually prepare this pastry in quantity, then store it in the freezer, wrapped in one-tart portions. That way, I'm always ready with a quick dessert for an unexpected dinner.

1½ cups flour
2 tablespoons sugar
Pinch salt
8 tablespoons (4 ounces) cold
   unsalted butter, cut up
1 egg yolk
1 tablespoon orange juice or
   cold water, plus more as
   needed

By Hand:
Sift together the flour, sugar and salt in a large bowl. Cut in the butter until crumbly; do not overmix.

Stir together the egg yolk and 1 tablespoon liquid in a small cup, and stir into the flour mixture with a fork. Add more liquid if necessary, until the pastry coheres into a ball. Do not make the dough too wet. Knead gently once or twice, then gather into a ball again.

Flatten the dough into a disk shape, wrap and chill at least 1 hour.

With Food Processor:
Place the dry ingredients in the processor; add the butter and pulse just until crumbly. Do not overprocess.

Transfer the mixture to a bowl and add liquid as described above. The pastry must not become overhomogenized. Brief handling is essential, or you will not achieve the ideal, slightly flaky tart crust.

Cookie Crust

This is based on a recipe of Professor Carlo Bussetti, a fine baker who was my teacher at New York City Community College.

16 tablespoons (8 ounces)
   unsalted butter, at room
   temperature
1 cup sugar
Pinch salt
Grated zest of 2 oranges
¼ cup lightly beaten egg
   (1 extra-large egg, or
   1 large egg plus 1 yolk)
2 tablespoons milk
2 teaspoons pure vanilla extract
2 cups cake flour (about 6 ounces)
1½ cups all-purpose flour (about
   6 ounces)

Cream the butter with an electric mixer. Add the sugar, salt and grated orange zest; beat until very fluffy. Beat in the egg, milk and vanilla, then lower the mixer speed and add the flours. Stop mixing as soon as the flour is mixed in. Do not overmix or the dough will be tough. The dough should be soft, but not sticky. Gather it together in a large bowl. Dust the dough with flour; wrap, and chill well.

Crème Fraîche

Makes about 2⅓ cups

This is a fair approximation of the thick cream used in France to make smooth sauces and luscious desserts. If you can find cream that is not ultra-pasteurized, it will be even better.

2 cups heavy cream
⅓ cup buttermilk

Combine the cream and buttermilk in a saucepan and heat just until warm, about body temperature (just under 100 degrees). Do not let it get hot.

Pour the mixture into a clean plastic or glass container and place the container, covered, in a larger container of warm water. The water should come up to the level of the cream.

Allow to stand in a warm place until thickened, about 12 to 36 hours. Replace the water every now and then to keep it warm. The timing will vary; on a hot summer day, the container of water may not even be necessary.

Refrigerate the container of cream; it will keep for about a week, and will become even thicker.